SINGING
in the
RAIN

52 Practical Steps to Happiness

Rachel Kelly

Disclaimer

The information in this book is not intended to replace or conflict with advice given to you by your GP or other health professional. All matters regarding your health should be directly discussed with your GP. The author and the publisher disclaim any liability directly or indirectly from the use of material in this book by any person.

Published in 2019 by
Short Books, Unit 316,
ScreenWorks, 22 Highbury Grove,
London N5 2ER

10 9 8 7 6 5 4 3 2 1

A CIP catalogue record for this book
is available from the British Library.

ISBN: 978-1-78072-358-7

Design © Smith & Gilmour
Cover illustrations © Jonathan Pugh 2019
Internal illustrations © Evie Dunne 2019

Printed by CPI Group (UK) Ltd, Croydon CR0 4YYW

For George

CONTENTS

Why my story led to *Singing in the Rain* p.6

NB! Look out for the smiley emoji ☺ for quick and easy exercises

Expanding your range

Hitting the higher notes

Why my story led to Singing in the Rain

This book was prompted by my own experience of being seriously unwell with depression. I am recovered now, but it hasn't always been like this. In my thirties, I suffered two major depressive episodes.

Both bouts of illness stemmed from doing too much and being overly busy, though I know others suffer from feeling their lives are empty. It all began one May when depression struck me seemingly out of the blue. I was taking our two small sons – a six-month-old baby and a toddler – upstairs for bath time. I laid them on their snow-white towels, kissing their rounded tummies in our normal routine, when my heart started racing.

That night I was gripped by insomnia. I thought I was having a heart attack; my heart was beating so wildly. I paced the house all night, checking and re-checking the children. When I lay in bed unable to sleep, my worries went round and round and I became increasingly overwhelmed. I was bursting with an active sense of dread that disaster was about to strike and I couldn't do anything to stop it. It felt like I was on a plane that was going to crash. In three days I went from being mildly anxious to being unable to move, in an agonising foetal curl on the floor, suicidal with fear.

This proved to be the start of my first major depressive episode, born of anxiety. I was briefly hospitalised, and was then ill for a further six months. I was treated with antidepressants and sleeping pills and eventually returned to work, hoping the problem would go away.

My luck held, but then I had a second breakdown several years later. That time, the trigger was something as seemingly insignificant as holding a Christmas get-together. Our house was full of family and friends for festive drinks. I had been trying to be the consummate hostess, twirling strangers together as if choreographing an elaborate dance. But my mistake was to pause briefly for breath in the kitchen amid the dirty glasses and empty trays. At that moment, I knew the battle was over. All the physical symptoms I recognised were back: the racing heart, the sense of dread, worries piling on worries. Once again, my fears solidified into harrowing physical symptoms. Once again, all I could do was lie in bed and scream. I was screaming because of the pain. Every bit of me was in acute, dynamic, physical agony. It felt as if I was back on a plane that was crashing, hurtling at high speed. That time I was ill for the best part of two years.

I probably had an underlying tendency to anxiety. I was a happy but sensitive child, and this combined with the acute societal pressure I felt to be good in every role I played – wife, journalist and mother. In the end I was overwhelmed, an experience I wrote about in my first book *Black Rainbow: How Words Healed Me – My Journey Through Depression*, published in 2014. My descent into depressive illness is a cautionary tale for all of us trying to juggle the multiple demands of work, family and our need for status and approval above our own emotional well-being and health. We need to tread warily amid the demands of modern life and the pressures we put on ourselves.

So I began to collect a toolkit of ideas for good mental health to make a third depressive episode less likely. It is a bit like breaking your arm. After a couple of breaks, you feel more vulnerable to a third. Aside from the main approaches prescribed by doctors for anxiety and depression – chiefly medication and therapy – I had every incentive to see if I could find other strategies for myself.

My first tool was, perhaps somewhat surprisingly, the healing power of words. When I was first ill I would hold on to my husband or mother to stop this terrifying sense of falling. My mother has a head filled with snippets of literature and inspiring quotations, as well as poetry. She would repeat lines of hope from poets like George Herbert who wrote: 'Who would have thought my shrivel'd heart/ Could have recovered greenness.' I would repeat them with her. I found it soothing to imagine I too would recover. The poetry provided a different, more positive narrative in my head.

As I got better, we moved to verses, and then entire poems. Short, accessible consolatory poems proved most helpful. I found other strategies helpful too. Exercise, mindfulness, therapy and especially nutrition all played their parts in my recovery, ideas I wrote about in my books *Walking on Sunshine: 52 Small Steps to Happiness* published in 2015, and *The Happy Kitchen: Good Mood Food*, published in 2017. I now have my Black Dog, as Winston Churchill used to describe his own depression, on a tight leash. Little by little, I have regained my health and returned to work and being a mother. I now feel positive much of the time, though of course I sometimes have a down day and still have much to learn about staying calm and peaceful.

While my earlier books have been more about the ideas I have found helpful, *Singing in the Rain* reflects more practical steps which I've found increasingly beneficial. It is a workbook full of things you can actually *do* for your wellbeing, be it writing a letter, drawing a picture, or making some origami, as well as stuff to try in the big bad world. Research shows that we regret what we don't do; thinking often makes me sad, but doing rarely does. A sense of my own autonomy and agency was essential to getting better. There's an easily won satisfaction in being active and occupied. As Confucius said: 'I hear and I forget, I see and might remember, I do and I understand.'

So there are lots of invitations to cut, colour and handle this book, and particularly to write stuff down. Picking up a pen might sound old-fashioned, but this is deliberate and has a basis in science. Research has found that writing about emotional experiences can boost our wellbeing, and can even make people's wounds heal more quickly. Noting things down has this magical ability to clarify our thoughts, and galvanise us into action. Writing is also an obvious way to have a tangible record of our thoughts and ideas and is a nice tonic to the transience of life.

If you really do work through the book, you will be left with something solid which feels real, rather than something lost to the digital ether.

In a world that's speeding up, thanks to social media and 24-hour news, and one in which instant gratification is central to our culture, the requirement to write Slows. Us. Down. I know I have had many more happy moments since I slackened my pace.

I learnt about many of the practical steps in the book from fellow sufferers of depression and those who helped me recover. For the last few years I have run workshops on wellbeing for mental health charities as well as in schools and for companies. Others have shared their thoughts online through my website and blog. Though some people naturally see the world in a positive way, I discovered that many think and worry like I do: I road-tested the ideas in *Singing in the Rain* with subscribers from my mailing list and volunteers who have come to my workshops. The book reflects all these different conversations and meetings.

These are my top 52 suggestions for practical steps to staying calm and well: one for each week of the year. Ideally spend a week on each one, but read the book as the fancy takes you. Dip in and out, and feel free to ignore any exercises or take more or less time, depending on what works for you. I do not advise reading the book at a sitting. No one could possibly absorb or appreciate quite so much advice all at once.

The activities are divided into four sections; think of it like learning to sing. Stage one is to warm up; stage two is to develop your voice; stage three is to expand your range; and stage four is to hit the higher notes.

At the start are my basics. Many of these are steps for physical wellbeing, given the link between mental and physical health. Adopt these practices, and you will build a solid foundation from which you can progress through to the more nuanced activities.

Then, as you go through the book, there is a wide range of exercises to choose from. Some of them may require more time and reflection, while other activities can be completed in a spare moment and are relatively quick fixes. The latter are marked on the contents page with the symbol of a smiley emoji.

After each section, there's a moment to pause and appreciate how far you have come. Here I am not asking you to do anything, just to draw a gentle breath and enjoy a pleasant thought. The nice news is that as you adopt new practical steps and change your thoughts and behaviour, your brain will change too. What we focus on expands, and we become what we pay attention to.

Just as a walker on a mountain path often takes the footpaths worn by others, your brain will take the path of least resistance when it comes to your habits.

You may have to make a real effort to break habits which are often biologically hardwired into us, but the old footpaths will slowly become redundant. In this way, the landscape of your mind is being altered. Hold on to this image of a well-worn path as you complete the activities in the book, creating new practical steps to happiness one by one.

I know I'm using the right wellbeing strategies for me when I am able to sing in the rain, or in other words, when I can see the positives within the negatives each day. I remember in particular one wet journey back from the Tube. I was soaked by the kind of horizontal rain that manages to get inside a zipped jacket and trickles down the back of your neck; my shoes squelching like mini paddling pools. Yet as I rounded the corner to our house, I saw our shaggy, golden-haired dog, Sammy on our doorstep, equally drenched, turning circles in delight at my return. Despite the darkening clouds, I spotted a tiny patch of cornflower blue. And I really did find myself humming 'doo-doo-doo-doo', even if I never will dance like Gene Kelly.

WARMING UP

1.

CENTERING YOURSELF

Every time I travel by plane, I am reminded that it is not selfish or navel-gazing to look after yourself: to take care of others we need to take care of ourselves. We all know the emergency instructions: put your own oxygen mask on first before you attend to those around you.

Begin by thinking of your life as a chunky black bicycle wheel. In the centre is you. The spokes radiating from the hub, meanwhile, are all the different aspects of your life, whether that includes a family, a job, your pet, a hobby, or your friends. If one of these spokes is damaged or falls off, your wheel, along with all the other spokes, will keep turning, as long as you have remained centred. If, however, you put something or someone other than yourself at the hub and it comes away, then the whole structure falls apart.

On the next page is a wheel to complete. If you can't fill in all the spaces between the spokes, don't worry, just colour or shade in any remaining ones. As valued as each of these aspects of your life are, this activity is about putting yourself in the centre to provide a stable framework.

A second way of feeling calm and centred is to remind yourself of your strengths. Typically, we are good at remembering what goes wrong in our lives, in the same way we remember criticism rather than praise. Our brains are designed this way. As animals, we have evolved to look out for danger and we are all descendants of those who tiptoed away from angry lions. Our modern kind of danger is internal and psychological, namely all that introspection and telling ourselves bad things. Let's begin by focusing on the positives instead. In the exercise that follows, note some of your strengths and recent compliments you have been given, which you may struggle to remember. This is about putting yourself first – in a good way. Typically, we tend to give out compliments readily but find it hard to absorb and receive them. Thus armed, you will be in a good frame of mind to complete the rest of the activities.

Your turn to put yourself first:

1. Fill in the bicycle wheel below, with the different aspects of your life in the spaces between the spokes.

Family   Friends

Work   Godchildren

YOU

Marriage

F1

Yoga   House-keeping

2. Next, write in the box below three strengths you like about yourself. Options could include your moral qualities, like being kind; characteristics such as being calm under pressure; or aspects of you for which you are grateful, like being able to swim, or run or dance, or make people laugh.

3. Split the following coat of arms into four sections. In each of the sections write a compliment that someone has given you. It could be the reason why you are a good partner or friend, or a detail that someone noticed about your work. Write a few words in each section.

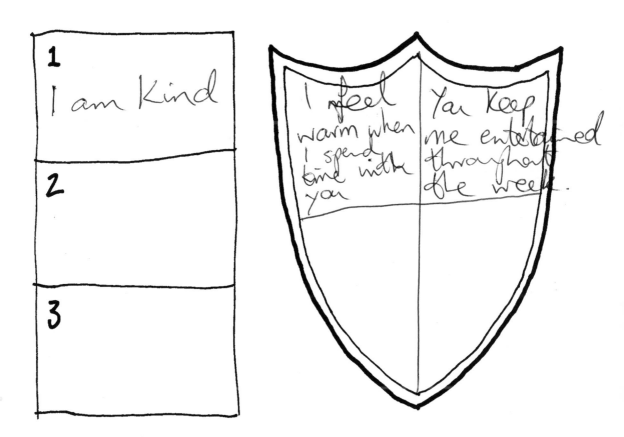

1

I am Kind

2

3

I feel warm when I spend time with you

You keep me entertained throughout the week.

② .

BELLY BREATHING

I find becoming aware of my breath is another way of feeling calm and centred, and such a good one that it's the second exercise I would like you to try. My preferred method is belly breathing, so called because it involves breathing deep into our stomachs, and becoming aware of the rise and fall of our diaphragm as we do so. I've found it among the easiest breathing techniques to master, perhaps because gently breathing deeply in this way is what we do naturally as babies. We are just re-learning something we have always known. Forget sleeping like a baby; just remember to breathe like one.

The exercise involves breathing through your nose rather than your mouth. Our noses are perfectly designed for the purpose: the little hairs in the nostrils filter out particles in the air and the chamber behind the nose cools or warms the air to the right temperature for our bodies.

The exercise also asks you to breathe out for longer than you breathe in. Exhalation is linked to the body's relaxation system and by breathing in this way we slow our heartbeat, stabilise or lower our blood pressure and increase our oxygen intake.

A good way to do this is to count to roughly seven as you breathe in, and 11 as you breathe out. You may have to adjust the number of seconds depending on your lung capacity and how practised you are: being small, I use shorter counts. But try and stick to using uneven numbers, so you are less likely to fall into an easy rhythm. This is important because you want to concentrate on your breathing, rather than switch into a rhythm and let your mind and its worries take over again.

Today, for example, I used belly breathing several times to deal with some stressful moments that peppered a difficult day. I received a text from a workmate cancelling a meeting; I lost my return train ticket on my way home; a colleague told me she found me difficult; and a company said they didn't want to collaborate on a project together.

At times like these, my fearful old brain systems are in danger of taking over: my past pattern would be to imagine worst-case scenarios. My breathing would become shallow and I would begin to sweat with a familiar prickly underarm feeling, the so-called stress response designed for acute physical emergencies, but which can be activated in our daily life. So I turn difficulty into catastrophe. Everybody hates me, my career is doomed and I'm going to face a hefty fine for losing my train ticket.

Now, I use belly breathing to stop my threat system in its tracks and to soothe me, giving my calmer, cognitive brain a chance to respond to stress in a more reasoned and sensible way. You can only breathe in the moment: you can't breathe in the past or the future, so it's a great way to avoid regrets or worries about what may happen. I also belly breathe when I am not stressed: studies show we are more focused and think straighter when we use breathing exercises.

Belly breathing today gave me the time to discover that my workmate had cancelled our meeting because she was unwell and we calmly rearranged another time; it allowed me the space to search through my bag properly and I found my ticket; it gifted me the calm to have a good chat with my colleague and to agree that while there were elements of our working relationship that we needed to address, other aspects were positive; and it gave me the strength to accept I would no longer be working with that company.

In all four scenarios, using belly breathing sent a safety signal to my nervous system that the threat I imagined was not true, and to move out of the involuntary danger response I had in place. Belly breathing tackles one of the most powerful and frightening symptoms of anxiety: the muscle tension in the chest, which makes our breathing uncomfortable. This tension also makes our thoughts spiral, so by belly breathing, we are creating the space to be here and now, and we can find better solutions to troubling problems – which is fitting, as the word 'inspire' actually means breathe in. A nice note on which to take a breath.

See also *Chanting, gargling and humming* on page 60.

Your turn to belly breathe:

First read through the instructions below so you know what you are doing, then lie down. If this is not possible, you can do the exercise sitting down, in which case you may prefer to put your hand on your stomach rather than use this book.

1. Put this book on your stomach.

2. Place your other hand on your chest.

3. Breathe in through your nose for a count of seven (or whatever you can manage).

4. As you do so, feel your stomach fill with air and push the book out as hard as you can.

5. Breathe out for the count of 11 (or whatever you can manage).

6. Feel your stomach deflate as you do so and observe the book move back down towards your diaphragm.

7. As you breathe out, you could also imagine you are breathing out any negative thoughts or stresses you may be experiencing.

8. Your hand on your chest should be as still as you can manage.

9. Repeat till you feel calmer.

3.

RISING EARLY

Picture the scene. You have just woken up an hour after you meant to. You start checking your emails in a panic. You have not eaten. You have spilled your coffee on your white shirt. You are even irritated by your dog nuzzling up to say hello (my own sure sign of grumpiness).

On bad mornings like these, I remind myself of the importance of having a positive frame of mind and a proper routine first thing. Cultivating this kind of morning freshness, or feeling *morgenfrisk* as the Danish rather charmingly put it, determines much of the rest of my day. The first step is not to be in a rush.

The easiest way to give myself a little more time in the morning has been to wake up earlier, which in addition is good for our health. Research shows early risers live longer. In addition, much of society and work is arranged around early birds.

Sleep scientists have taught us that there are two types of sleepers: larks and owls. Some of us are owls (good at staying up late) and some of us are larks (good at getting up early). And, of course, some of us are somewhere in between (if

any reader can think of a bird to describe these people in the middle, please tweet me @RachelKellyNet).

I am definitely an owl. Being an owl is like being left-handed in a right-handed world. And gosh, I have found it hard to adjust to being more of a lark, as these habits are pretty hardwired. Rather than feeling bad about not being able to make the switch, see if you can at least recognise your own tendencies and make some adjustments, even small ones. It may take more than the week I usually allot to build this habit.

Here are some suggestions to help you make the switch to becoming an earlier and calmer riser. First, spring or summer is probably the best time to transition, as it's when the light will be waiting to greet you when you wake a little earlier. Then reset your clock for an earlier morning wake-up each day rising five minutes earlier than the day before, till you reach your target wake-up time. It took me a couple of weeks to adjust to waking an hour or so earlier. It's hard to recommend exactly what that time should be as we are all different and experience varying demands. One rule of thumb is to mimic roughly the natural pattern of light and dark, which means the optimal bedtime is around 10 p.m. and the optimal wake-up time is around 6 a.m. to align broadly with the summer sun's setting and rising.

In the morning, think of waking as a process rather than as an instant occurrence completed at high speed before you get out of the door. I know I always feel at my most raw when I stir. As the day progresses, I feel as if I put on protective layers, but first thing I am often fearful. So I have now added in some time to my morning routine for breathing and stretching, which make me feel grounded. As does making my bed. (See also *Taking back control* on page 155). You may find it motivating to think of other things you can do with the extra time, whether it is something creative or watching the sunrise.

On which note... Expose yourself to daylight as soon as you can. The more light you get in the morning, the more your body clock speeds up. This in turn should make you feel more tired at the end of the day, and ready for sleep that bit earlier. Remember the hours before midnight are especially restful: it's called

midnight for the reason that for many, it used to be the mid-point of their night's sleep.

Rising early is also a useful approach to insomnia, which so often accompanies anxiety. Try not to worry about being awake at night. It is the worrying that is so debilitating, rather than the lack of sleep itself.

Continue to make your morning easier by not reaching for your phone. Emails are best left unanswered until you are at your desk and in full work mode. Then, coax yourself through the next bit of the morning by making breakfast enticing: some golden scrambled eggs and a jet-black espresso with just a froth of creamy white milk in my case.

Once you have shifted to an earlier start, don't change your wake-up time dramatically just because it's the weekend or you have had a bad night's sleep (as I sometimes do). Our hormones love regularity. A weekend 'jet lag' effect can build up if we succumb to a lie in, however tempting it may seem.

Regular habits, both at the beginning and end of day make sense, not just for me but for Sammy too.

Your turn to become more of a lark and less of a night owl by recording your efforts:

Decide on your new target wake-up time that you will reach by the end of two weeks and record it in the star. Each day adjust your wake-up time by roughly five minutes till you reach your target.

WEEK 1			WEEK 2		
day of week	target wake-up time	I made my morning easier and more pleasant by...	day of week	target wake-up time	I made my morning easier and more pleasant by...

4.

DRESSING

Today it is time for a wardrobe clear-out. Along with some moth-eaten winter woollens, I am making a pile of anything white that has turned grey, and anything that is frayed, beyond repair or no longer fits. Stuff which is still wearable goes in a pile for charity, as someone else can benefit and it is nice to think they might do so. This bit is easy. It's trickier to know, of all the clothes that remain, which ones I should value and treasure.

Clothes are partly about showing respect for others, even if this fact of life is hard for many to accept. With what we wear, we send a message that we have made an effort, and that in turn we are worth making an effort for. But clothes are also about how we feel on the inside, which is true whatever gender we are. I remember asking a psychotherapist why she dressed with care. 'Our inner selves are reflected in our outward appearance, and vice versa,' she explained. 'I can usually tell my clients' state of mind by how they dress.'

So my wardrobe clear-out is dictated by how clothes make me feel. What we wear does indeed reflect our mood, but equally we can change that mood by how we dress. We wear our clothes, but our clothes wear us. The poet John Keats supposedly used to put on his smartest suit before he wrote to help him focus and create a sense of occasion.

In the past I often used to read the wisdom of fashion pundits. Now I am wary of those who proclaim what we should or shouldn't wear. I hate rules such as 'you must keep your hair short past forty' or 'ruffles are a mistake at any age'. In fact I love ruffles and don't think there is any reason why age should determine hairstyle. Individual style is just that – individual.

My own strategy is to be more attentive to whether clothes make me feel relaxed and authoritative, both at work and home. For this to happen, an obvious starting point is that everything ideally needs to be clean, with no lose threads, collapsing hems or missing buttons. I say ideally, as I sometimes rush out of the house only to discover my clothes are none of these things. I have also become more aware of how wearing something colourful boosts my morale – I now favour a ruby red jacket and a pair of powder pink jeans. Another top-scoring sartorial item for improving my mood are immaculately bright white shirts. I cherish them as they always make me feel better about myself but only if they are properly white which explains today's clear-out.

Now I have found the clothes that improve my mood in this way, I keep a record of them by drawing stick women and scribbling details of the outfits alongside them. It may not be quite as powerful as having a dresser like the

Queen, but this kind of advance planning means that I am less stressed if I am in a rush to get dressed (remember our peaceful mornings). For some, stress-free dressing may mean developing something of a uniform: Angela Merkel has the same cut of suit in numerous colours, while Apple co-founder Steve Jobs was famous for his black turtlenecks.

When I wear my tried and tested friends, somehow I find myself smiling, which is the ultimate accessory. What clothes do you value and treasure?

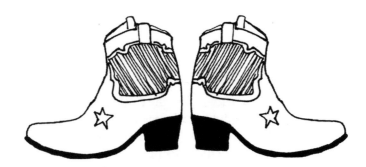

Your turn to use your clothing to change your mood:

1. Think of the outfit you are wearing right now. Answer the following questions in the space below.

2. Does what you are wearing make you feel relaxed and authoritative? Boost your mood? Is your outfit clean with no loose threads or buttons or collapsing hems?

....

....

....

....

3. Gradually edit your cupboard accordingly, or do a clear-out in one go.

4. On the figures opposite, draw the clothes in which you feel most confident to remind you when you are struggling to find something to wear or, if you would rather, write notes by the side of the figures. You could stick in photos of your outfits if you prefer.

5. Now, if you can, try on one of your outfits. Accessorise with a smile, of which more next...

My top mood-boosting outfits include:

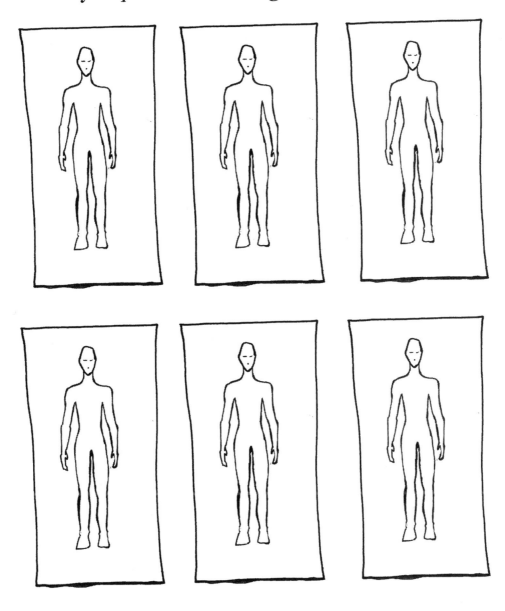

(5.)

SMILING AND LAUGHING

My niece is still at that delightful age when she laughs at her own jokes. She recently shared a few of her latest offerings: how many tickles does it take to make an octopus laugh? Ten-tickles. Why did the bicycle fall over? Because it was two tired. Even though the jokes were questionable, her laughter was infectious.

It's not just fun to laugh. It's also important for our wellbeing and has plenty of benefits. As it says in Proverbs in the King James's version of the Bible, 'A merry heart doeth good like a medicine: but a broken spirit drieth the bones.'

First, laughter can help us get over our worries. I remember my cousin saying she knew I would be happy with my future husband because he made me chuckle and what was joy if not laughter? When I was depressed, he would ask me to list all my worries. Which I did. After each one he would say 'Next', until we got to the point when I couldn't think of any more concerns. Then he would say triumphantly, 'See, no more worries!' I would chortle despite my best efforts not to.

Laughter reduces anxiety as it is the ultimate release into the moment: you can only laugh in the now (though of course you can guffaw while reflecting on the past). It allows you to put things into perspective. Next time you are frightened of someone, try and giggle at something about them. It's an immediate equaliser, although best done privately.

Second, laughter can help us bond with others. Originally, we grouped together to give us protection from predators. This makes us social animals. Our brains treat being accepted by others as a matter of life or death.

The same is true today. We like being part of groups. Which explains why laughter is so contagious: it affirms that we belong. Smiling changes how people react to you (for the better).

More laughter equals more wellbeing. My own strategies for laughing more include spending time with little children, as I did with my niece, and remembering amusing times. But probably the most effective way I laugh more is to smile more. This lowers the bar, as most of us can smile relatively easily at will, and in turn smiling is often a gateway to laughing.

When we adopt an outwardly glum expression, our old reptilian brains imagine a threat. By contrast, when we smile or enjoy a warm facial expression, we activate what scientists call our 'soothing system': the emotional system which leaves us feeling content and joyful, even when we smile on our own.

The trick is to smile with your eyes and not just your mouth. You'll find that the minute you smile at someone else, they are apt to reciprocate. You can even keep a record of how often you smile at others. Laughter may soon follow, with or without the help of any octopus jokes.

Your turn to get serious about smiling and laughing:

1. To smile more:

   ● Look at this sketch of the Mona Lisa painting.

   ● Relax your face and copy her expression.

   ● Feel a gentle half smile on your lips.

   ● Breathe gently, relax the small muscles around your eyes and notice how it feels to smile with your eyes. Imagine the smile flowing through your body, bathing it in warmth and light.

   ● Now you are smiling, go and smile at the next person you see and see if they don't reciprocate. You will probably find you are drawn to others who seem light-hearted and content and who are already smiling.

2. Use the daily smile chart below. Turn the empty circles below into smiley faces for each person you smile at per day. Try and smile at two or three new people a day for the next week, as well as those you already know.

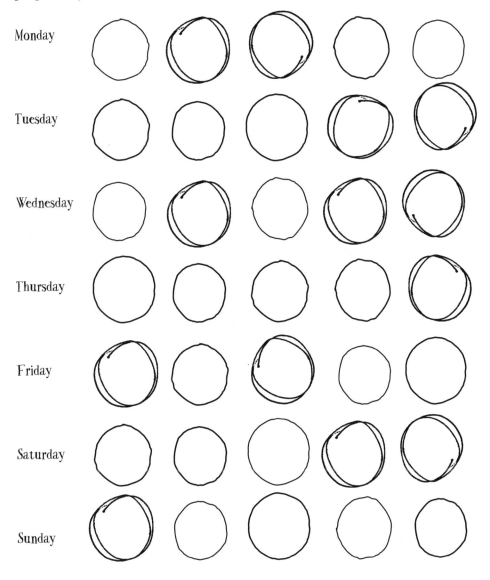

Monday

Tuesday

Wednesday

Thursday

Friday

Saturday

Sunday

3. Recall in greater detail some happy memories. For example, what are some funny things your friends or family have said? When was the last time you laughed at yourself? What is the funniest joke you have ever told? Who were you with? Where and when did they happen? Recalling these times may spark a smile.

WHAT?	WHO?	WHERE & WHEN?

6.

VISUALISING

One way I have learnt to manage my stress levels has been to use mental imagery – to create or experience visual pictures in the mind. These images can help us understand and become aware of our moods, be they high or low, as well as control them. Cancer sufferers also use this method to help them relax and manage their symptoms.

Visualisations naturally evoke our sense of sight, and can become more vivid still when we add in our other senses. Imagine what sounds, smells or tactile sensations might accompany the pictures. Although visualising something is not equivalent to experiencing it in the real world, the process can still produce the same physical response. If you are ever tempted to question the mind-body connection, try visualisation. Our imaginations are powerful indeed.

The following are two images I use to first gauge and then manage my mood.

First, the pendulum. This could be a stone, weight or crystal hanging from the end of a string, but in our case imagine it is this very book (see overleaf for how to turn it into a pendulum). When I am calm, I imagine that the string is still, the book peacefully at the end of it, not moving to right or left. This is the happy middle ground, when I am in balance, neither too high nor too low. But when I get either overly stressed or overly excited, the book starts to swing from side to side – a useful visual representation to remind me of my own mood swings.

Then at times when I feel really unstable, I imagine the book swinging so fast it is out of control. This image reminds me I have little perspective, and can quickly become either upset and angry, or by contrast on too much of a high. The picture in my head is a reminder that I need to pause. I must find a way to calm down and return to the mid-point.

Using the pendulum image has helped me become more aware of my mood swings. I have learnt that it is better not to act when I feel so out of control, as I will almost certainly regret it. I also use this image as a way to disconnect from the feelings it represents. By observing the pendulum, I watch my emotional volatility rather than 'becoming' it.

The second image is of a vast expanse of sky above me. Thinking about this is a way I return to feeling peaceful and safe. I imagine that my challenging thoughts and emotions are like small, passing clouds. Just as clouds aren't solid, nor are my thoughts and emotions, however difficult they feel at that moment. I can choose to let my feelings pass gently by, just as the clouds do. And, however dark the clouds maybe, beyond them the sky is pale blue and infinite. The spaciousness of the sky makes me feel as if there is more room in my head for all these tricky feelings.

Working with these two images in this sequence makes me feel more powerful. I am the one who has gauged and understood my anxiety, and brought my own stress levels down. Thanks to my pendulum and my sky, I am able to tackle whatever is stressing me in a calm and positive way.

Your turn to use the power of imagery:

The pendulum
You can either just imagine the pendulum image, or you can actually turn this book into a pendulum by following the steps below, which means you need to find some string.

1. Lay a piece of string along the spine inside this book, leaving extra on each side.

2. Tie the two sides of string together to form a triangle with the book dangling below.

3. Swing the book from side to side.

4. Slowly allow the swinging to speed up, as your mood swings from high to low and back again.

5. Let the book gradually slow down and stop swinging, as it tries to find the balanced mid-point.

6. Imagine yourself calming down at the same time, returning to the peaceful middle ground rather than the highs or lows.

7. If you have not physically turned this book into a pendulum, imagine all the steps above to summon up the image in your mind.

2. The sky

Summon up an image of the sky. You may want to go outside, or if you can't, go near a window so you can see the sky.

Can you hear any birds?

How does the air feel?

Can you feel its warmth?

Are you experiencing any other tactile sensations?

Imagine the pale blue above the clouds that you can't see.

Enjoy a sense of spaciousness.

Imagine the clouds passing, just as stressful moments will pass.

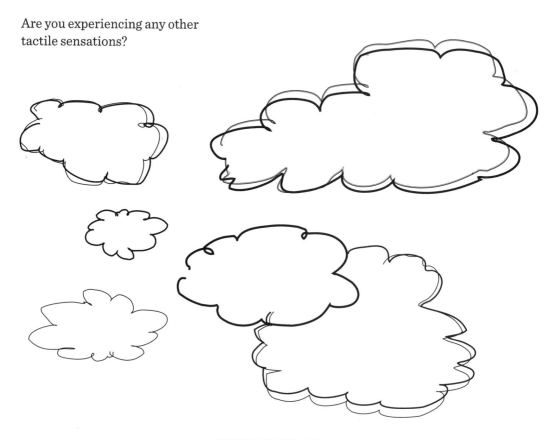

7.

MOVING

I went to see *Billy Elliot: The Musical* at the weekend and one scene in particular resonated with me. It's the moment where the young would-be ballet star Billy describes what dancing feels like.

Once I get going I forget everything
I sort of disappear
Like I feel a change in my whole body
Like there's fire in my body
I am just there, flying like a bird
Like electricity...

Of course, I will never dance like Billy, but I do know what he means about feeling the fire in our bodies when we engage in vigorous exercise. Evidence suggests we need this kind of energetic exertion to boost low mood. The problem is, not everyone wants to get hot and sweaty and not everyone can find the time. I aim for bursts of intense exercise a few times a week. For me this translates into cycling up the hill near my house. I pedal for around 20 seconds, after which the pain is so intense that I have to stop. One day I will get to the top.

The NHS recommends 150 minutes of moderate aerobic exercise a week, such as cycling or brisk walking. To feel the psychological benefit you should build up to this level of physical activity.

We also need other, more sedate types of exercise we can slot into our day, like walking. I call this kind of exercise 'movement' which feels less threatening.

Take this week. Instead of meeting in an office or café, a colleague and I decided to have a 'walk 'n' talk' meeting. Our conversation flowed easily as we ambled side by side. In that one trip we achieved more than in several more formal get-togethers in the office. Exercise isn't just about our physical health, our appearance or our weight. It's about feeling happy in ourselves. Our conversation mirrored how I felt: grounded, stable and positive.

Adding in some walking to your day can make a difference. Enjoy the experience more by becoming attentive to the process of walking itself: the feel of the pavement under your feet, or the way your leg moves as you take a stride. And if more walking proves tricky? Remember it is easier than biking up the hill.

Your turn to incorporate more movement into your day:

1. Draw a rough sketch of your place of work in the box opposite. You might include your desk, where the nearest bin is, the nearest toilet, the stairs or the lift, where meetings are held and where you have your lunch. Then annotate your sketch with notes on how you can introduce more walking into your workplace. (If you are based at home, you can adapt the drawing to reflect your home environment, and annotate the sketch in a similar way.) Here are some ideas to choose from:

- Take the stairs
- Have a walking meeting
- Walk or stand when you take phone calls
- Walk to the toilets furthest away from you
(maybe on the floor above or below)
- When you boil the kettle, do a lap of your office or house

2. Write on the path in between your home and work any points where you could add in extra movement, maybe by swapping public transport for cycling or walking, both on the way there and the way back. You could get off the bus, tube or train one stop earlier and walk the rest of the way.

3. Add in any points on your journey where you can include some high-intensity exercise. Mark them on your journey. Perhaps best on the way home so you can shower on arrival. If you are based at home, note any journeys you could take away from the house and where you could add in extra movement.

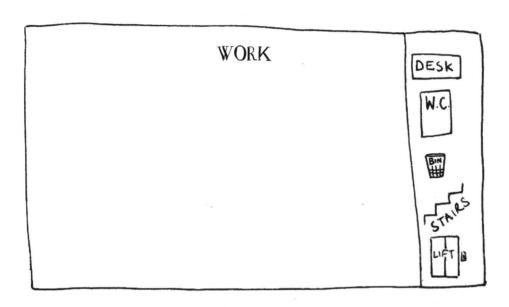

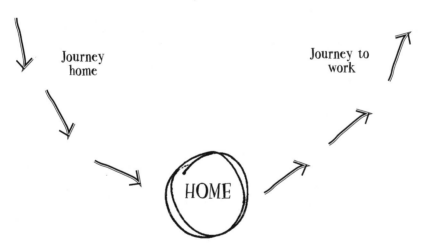

(8.)

EATING FOR CALM AND FOCUS

Be it summer, when we need to be the dreaded 'beach-body ready', or New Year when we need to shed the excess pounds we have gained over Christmas, it is hard to open a newspaper or magazine without reading about enticing new diets that promise a slimmer physique. Yet I have avoided these kinds of diets for a while now.

That's not to say I am not careful about what I eat and, indeed, how I eat it. I am. But my diet is not about losing weight. Rather, it's about eating for happiness and in particular about eating to reduce my stress levels. Alice Mackintosh is a registered nutritional therapist with whom I have worked for more than five years now. She says that if I feel stressed, I should concentrate on eating foods that boost four minerals and vitamins: magnesium, zinc, B vitamins and Vitamin C.

Magnesium supports our all-important adrenal glands, which control our response to stress. I have gone so far as to grow some spinach myself, as it is one of the best sources of magnesium, along with almonds, avocadoes and pumpkin seeds. I love the small, deep green leaves growing

bigger and stronger on our kitchen windowsill in their silvery trough.

Zinc assists with many functions, especially in the central nervous system, where it helps build new cells and enzymes. It is also thought to help brain cells communicate and to heighten concentration. Studies have linked zinc deficiency with depression and reduced focus. Top sources? Eggs, quinoa, chickpeas and mushrooms.

Having enough B vitamins is also linked to staying steady: Vitamin B5 supports our adrenal glands; Vitamin B9 and Vitamin B12 can boost mood; and Vitamin B6 can reduce anxiety. It is tricky to know which foods to recommend, as there are so many different forms of B vitamin. Wholegrains, meat, fish, seeds, nuts, pulses, beans and eggs are good sources but given that B vitamins occur in so many different foods, I like taking a B multivitamin.

Finally, Vitamin C. We can't store this water-soluble vitamin and need to make sure we get enough of it, as it is quickly used up when we are under stress. It helps us absorb iron, maintain our cartilage, bones and teeth, and supports our immune system. Colourful vegetables, fruit and fresh herbs and spices are great sources, including strawberries, kiwi, broccoli, oranges and the humble potato.

Alice offers other suggestions to reduce stress at mealtimes, including eating with someone else and being mindful while eating. I try to do this by appreciating what I have in front of me and savouring every sip or bite. She also recommends the power of staying hydrated and positive drinking in the form of a calming smoothie.

A keen amateur runner told me that when she meets up with her fellow sprinters at an athletics club, their coaches test them on their heart rates, their body weight, the number of hours they slept and the quality of their sleep. Their urine meanwhile is tested for urea and hydration levels. Of all these tests, which do the coaches think is the most important as the key measure for the body's readiness to perform? The answer is, perhaps surprisingly, the hydration scores.

We may not all be champion athletes, but we can learn from them the importance of drinking more water. Studies show that dehydration can impair mental functioning and cause changes in mood, as well as reductions in alertness, and short-term memory. Basically, the minute we aren't hydrated enough, our entire body feels stressed.

Our bodies are predominantly made up of water, so it naturally follows that all of our organs and tissues need to remain well hydrated to function smoothly. The amount of water you need depends on a number of factors, including the temperature, whether you have exercised and your age, though the general recommendation is 1.5 litres of fluid a day, which is around six to eight glasses of water. The easiest way to tell if you are dehydrated is by checking the colour of your urine. It should be pale, not dark yellow.

Time for a glass of water and one of Alice's Blissful Berry Smoothies. That is dietary advice I can follow whatever the time of year.

See also *Socialising and friendships* on page 86.

Your turn to eat and drink for calm:

Tick the ingredients you will buy this week to up your supplies of magnesium, zinc and vitamin C (in addition to taking a B multivitamin). You can use this table as a tool to incorporate a sufficient amount of these minerals into your diet. You might even consider growing your own vegetables.

MAGNESIUM RICH	VITAMIN C RICH	ZINC RICH
Men need 300mg a day Women need 270mg a day	All adults need 40mg of Vitamin C a day	Men need 9.5mg of zinc a day Women need 7mg of zinc a day
Spinach (1 cup contains around 24mg of magnesium)	Potatoes (1 cooked, skinned medium potato contains around 30mg of Vitamin C)	Dark chocolate (a 100g bar contains around 3mg of zinc)
Flaxseeds (1 tablespoon contains around 40mg of magnesium)	Strawberries (1 strawberry contains around 7mg of Vitamin C)	Eggs (1 egg contains around 0.5mg of zinc)
Pumpkin seeds (1 cup contains around 168mg of magnesium)	Green peppers (1 pepper contains around 95.7mg of Vitamin C)	Quinoa (1 cup contains around 2mg of zinc)
Almonds (10 almonds contain around 32mg of magnesium)	Kiwis (1 kiwi contains around 64mg of Vitamin C)	Chickpeas (1 cup contains around 2.5mg of zinc)
Avocado (1 avocado contains around 58mg of magnesium)	Oranges (1 medium-sized orange contains around 70mg of Vitamin C)	Mushrooms (1 cup contains around 1mg of zinc)

All figures from the NHS – for those aged between 19 and 64 plus

RECIPE FOR A CALMING SMOOTHIE:

Serves 1

$1/2$ banana
Large handful of stawberries (can be
    frozen)
Large handful of kale, thick stalks removed
$1/2$ avocado
6 almonds, or 1 teaspoon almond butter
200ml unsweetened almond milk (use less
    or more depending on desired consistency)

Pop all the ingredients into a food
processor and blend until smooth. This is
best enjoyed right away, but it can be kept
in the fridge for up to a day as an easy
snack or breakfast.

Some ways to improve hydration:

1. Keep a jug of water on the desk or kitchen table and add orange or lemon slices, cucumber and some mint sprigs to make it tastier.

2. Avoid caffeine after 4 p.m.

3. Use a colourful, fancy water bottle.

4. Have a glass of water by your bed and drink it when you wake up.

5. Eat more watery vegetables such as cucumber, carrots, celery, radishes, lettuce, cauliflower and leafy greens.

6. Eat more watery fruit such as kiwis, watermelons and grapefruit. An added bonus is these foods contain plenty of other minerals and vitamins, as well as fibre for good gut health.

7. Drink more herbal teas.

8. Write in the jug opposite the hydration tips that you are most likely to adopt. Then cut the image out, keep it somewhere handy, such as stuck on a fridge door, to remind yourself throughout the day of how to stay hydrated.

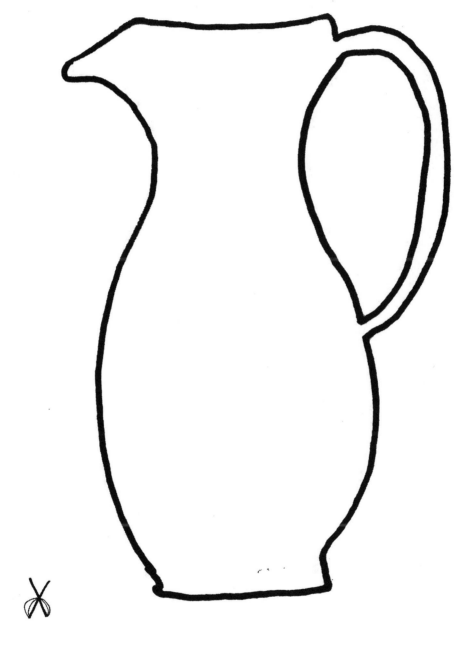

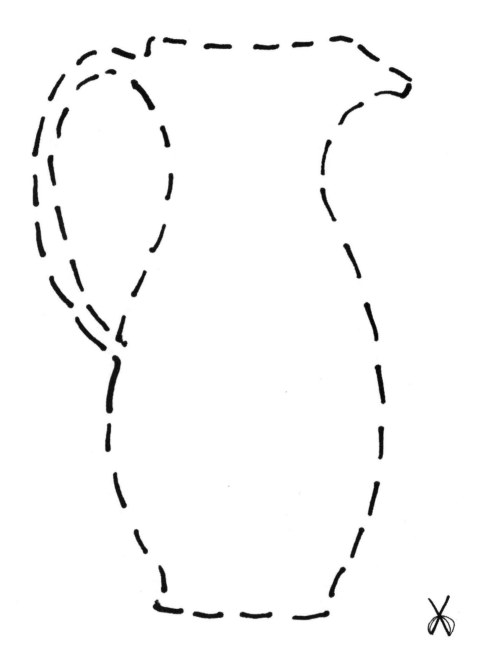

SINGING IN THE RAIN
42

9.

SITTING AND STANDING

When was the last time you stood, or sat up, to your full height – with poise, balance and ease? Stop for a minute now and observe your postural habits. If you are anything like me, you may have a stiff neck, tight hamstrings and a sore back. Unfortunately, many of us have become *homo computerensis*. We spend our days crouched over our desks, shoulders bent, as if protecting ourselves from some hidden threat.

Yet when we adopt a confident, open, upright pose, whether we are walking or sitting, we feel relaxed. Instead of being stuck both physically and mentally, everything flows more naturally. Because, actually, sitting does not come easily to us. We are taught to sit still as children, and our backs become rounded, causing unnecessary curvature and pain.

Knowing how my posture affects my mood has meant that I now consciously stand taller throughout my day. I spread my feet out, drop my shoulders and imagine a piece of string coming from the top of my head, with someone gently pulling me up, lengthening my back. I learnt how to do this from a teacher who practises the Alexander Technique, developed by Frederick Alexander in the 1890s.

It's also good for our posture to keep moving. I like kicking my shoes off and walking barefoot. It calms me and makes me feel grounded. (See also *Moving* on page 33).

Meanwhile, I have learnt to sit back in my chair for proper support – with my legs uncrossed and my knees at roughly a 120-degree angle: the higher you sit, the better for your posture. Crucially, my knees are lower than my hips, as this angle means my core muscles are activated. My spine is aligned. My shoulders are relaxed. I can feel the sitting bones at the base of my pelvis. My screen is an arm's length away, and the top of the screen is roughly eye level, which because of my desk height means it sits on several large books. And I enjoy stretching while at my desk too.

This may all sound difficult, and it is at first. But the good news is that the more you sit, stand and move in these ways, the more these habits will become lodged in your muscle memory. Soon good posture will become second nature to you. And it will help in ways you might not imagine.

Your turn to adopt a helpful body posture and to try out some stretches:

Read through the steps below first, and then when you are ready:

- Kick off your shoes.

- Stand with the balls of your feet and your toes flat on the floor.

- Release any tension in your tummy muscles.

- Allow an expansion on the in breath and a contraction on the out breath of your abdomen and rib cage so you are exercising your abdominal muscles and back just by the way you breathe.

- Drop your shoulders, letting go of any tension, and think of your arms as loose and heavy. Allow them to hang easily.

- Become aware of the earth beneath you and the air above you.

- Notice any tension in your body and allow it to flow out into the ground.

- For the rest of the day become more aware of your feet touching the floor.

- Resolve to repeat this helpful body posture every 45 minutes or so.

You can also use these stretching techniques to improve
your posture whilst sitting or standing:

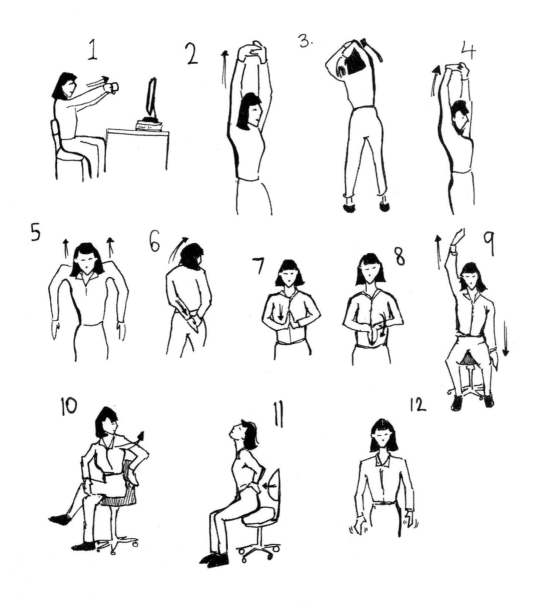

(10.)

RELAXING PHYSICALLY

A tense body means a tense mind. Equally, if you are physically relaxed, it is impossible to be anything other than mentally relaxed. Relaxing our muscles calms the central nervous system, reduces the production of adrenaline and directs oxygen away from an overly active brain.

On those days when I can't control my racing thoughts and struggle to relax my mind, it is a relief to approach the problem a different way by relaxing my body instead. Less a case of mind over body, more body over mind.

Yet much of our lives alienates us from our physical selves – we live in our heads and store tension and fear in our muscles. We can see this in the way mammals shake themselves all over to rid themselves of tension and stress after they escape from a predator.

Luckily, we can become re-connected with our bodies, and more appreciative of all they do for us. You might like to imagine that your body has emotions and needs to be cared for, almost as if it were a separate entity. A good way to do so is to embrace your physicality with specific poses for relaxation.

One good exercise is to deliberately become rigid and stiff, with tense shoulders and clenched fists for a few seconds, and then relax. To take this further, try the yoga wind-down positions, Child's Pose and Rock n' Roll: details of how to do these are on the next page. One study found that people who practised yoga for an hour experienced an increase in levels of GABA, a brain chemical linked to calm, compared with a zero increase within a control group, who read for an hour instead.

Another relaxing exercise is to slacken all of the body's muscle groups, one by one. I like to get comfortable somewhere and then mentally run through each muscle group in turn. By telling myself the muscle is relaxed, it then softens.

Thinking about my body and movement in this way has been a departure for me. Until recently, whenever I thought about physical activity, I imagined the cardio-vascular, heart-pumping, sweat-dripping kind – although this is important for our moods too, as I have discussed on page 33 in my *Moving* chapter.

My new enthusiasm is for physical activity more closely linked to my emotional self. The focus required for my relaxation exercises means I can't worry about anything else whilst I am doing them. I have included some of my favourite poses on the next page.

Joining a yoga class is next on my list, but meanwhile, I bow to you. Or, as they say in Sanskrit, namaste.

Your turn to use your body to relax your mind with some poses and a body scan:

Before you begin...

Tense your shoulders, scrunch up your face and make your hands into fists for ten seconds. Notice how stressed this pose makes you feel. Now release, and try these poses for contrast.

1. Child's pose

● Kneel on a mat or rug.

● Bring your knees together, lower your buttocks onto your feet and lean forward to rest your torso on your knees, so your forehead touches the mat. A variation of this, which many prefer, is to open out your knees which means your chest is lowered in the space between them.

● Place your arms alongside and behind you or outstretched in front of you for an extra back stretch.

● Be aware of your breathing.

2. Rock n' roll

● Lie down with your back straight and your arms resting slightly away from your body. Support your back with a small cushion or rolled-up towel if necessary.

● Bring your knees to your chest and put your arms around your shins, or thighs if easier.

● Keeping your spine in contact with the floor, roll your knees over to the right and then to the left, and then move your knees around in a gentle circular movement.

● Be aware of your breathing throughout.

● Relax your body into the floor as you rock and roll. Be aware of yourself alone, in this moment.

● Stay aware of your breathing. Release your legs and gently lower one and then the other to the ground.

● Rest.

3. The body scan

● Visualise the image of a body in your mind's eye.

● Keeping this image in your head, focus on the feet, and notice how your own feet are feeling.

● Repeat to yourself silently inside, 'my toes are relaxing, my toes are now relaxed' – this is a method called 'auto-suggestion' this is developed by the psychologist Émile Coué.

● Begin moving your mind's eye up through your heels, ankles, and on up your calves towards your knees. Again, notice each of your muscle groups in turn, and tell yourself each time that the particular muscle group is relaxing, the muscles are now relaxed.

● Now move up both thighs to the pelvic area and then slowly up to the waist. Keep releasing each muscle group, and keep silently telling yourself that you are relaxing, the muscles are now relaxed.

● Then slowly shift your focus to your hands and up your arms to your elbows, armpits and shoulders. Keep silently talking to yourself, telling yourself that you are relaxing, the muscles are now relaxed.

● After your shoulders, focus on your torso, traveling upwards from the waist, to the rib cage, chest and back. Keep talking quietly about how you are feeling relaxed, the muscles are now relaxed.

● Now move up to your neck, then face, through to the top of your head. Keep talking quietly about how these muscles are relaxing, they are now relaxed.

● Then reverse the flow of attention and go all the way back through the muscle groups from your head to your toes. Enjoy the feeling of your body sitting comfortably and the warm relaxation as you release all your muscle groups in turn and talk to yourself as you do so.

● Notice how focusing on your body also relaxes your mind. Use this relaxation whilst lying in bed to get to sleep, or any other time you would like to relax.

ENJOYING SIMPLE PLEASURES

One of my simple pleasures is scraping the chocolate froth off the top of a cappuccino in my local café. It's a small delight that sets my heart beating that little bit faster and one I try to incorporate into my day: I imagine I have been given a coupon, as if I have won a small prize. This gives me licence to enjoy myself, for no other reason than that something gives me a moment of joy.

This might sound rather self-indulgent. It's true we need purposeful activities such as working and learning in our lives. But having fun and being attuned to life's simple pleasures isn't selfish. As we established at the start of this book, by looking after ourselves and increasing our own sense of joy, we can reach out more easily to others. Cherishing the importance of small, ordinary things is a nice antidote to a world where sometimes it feels as if only what is intense, exceptional or transformative is valued.

Spend a little time working out what your simple pleasures really are. Consider how you might think, feel or behave to yourself if you were a caring friend. It is easy to believe we should enjoy something because that is what is expected of us, or even because it is what we expect of ourselves, rather than take a moment to examine what we really desire. In the words of Paul Dolan, Professor of Behavioural Science at LSE, we sometimes misjudge our enjoyment of activities. Plot a diary of what you did yesterday to pay more attention to any misconceptions you may have about what really makes you happy. For a period I thought I liked gossiping, until I realised it also made me feel guilty also. My son recently asked me to remove the computer in the kitchen. He had spent most of the weekend gaming, his greatest joy, so he thought. But then he realised he felt lousy afterwards.

Assuming you have correctly identified what truly sparks joy in your life, make an effort to notice these good times instead. Think of them as stop-and-savour moments. And make the magic last longer by giving yourself an extra second or two to focus and take a mental photograph of that moment, deliberately lingering on what can otherwise feel transient by making it into a ritual.

Allow yourself the time to feel exactly where you are enjoying the experience physically, checking in to your different senses: give consideration to the combination of the sweet chocolate and the taste of the espresso underneath, for example; or the warmth of the cup as you hold it in your hands; or the smell of the coffee beans infusing the café.

Then, spend a moment reflecting on the purpose such moments can give to our lives. Simple pleasures are not just material: you might feel less alone as you begin your day because when you decided to go for a coffee you gave yourself time to be open to the care and kindness of others, in this case the welcoming barista in a coffee shop. We can miss receiving kindness from others by being in a perpetual rush ourselves.

Or you might enjoy the feeling that you are looking after yourself and are worthy of a treat.

Thinking through a little more about the reason behind a simple pleasure will make it register in your brain. You might even imagine your brain forming a new neural pathway, as your mood lifts, one cup of coffee at a time.

See also *Being kind to others* on page 70.

Your turn to identify, assess and savour simple pleasures:

Fill in this form to evaluate what really makes you happy by listing small pleasurable things you did last week. Analyse whether each activity really did make you happy, and if it gave you a sense of purpose.

Activity	With whom?	For how long?	Pleasure it gave me (0-10)	Purpose I felt whilst doing it (0-10)

Each of these coupons entitles you to one simple pleasure. Choose one per day. Below are some coupons with suggested ideas, and then over the page there are some blank coupons for you to add in your own simple pleasures.

You could cut out the coupons, put them into a box, and then pick one out each day for an element of surprise if you prefer.

Enjoy each step of the new habits you will be creating. Hold on to that happy feeling and make it stick.

This coupon entitles you to: A £1 BUNCH OF DAFFODILS T&Cs: Must be savoured	This coupon entitles you to: A TAKEAWAY COFFEE T&Cs: Must be savoured	This coupon entitles you to: A WALK IN THE COUNTRYSIDE T&Cs: Must be savoured	This coupon entitles you to: A HOME-COOKED MEAL TO BRING INTO THE OFFICE AT LUNCH T&Cs: Must be savoured
This coupon entitles you to: SLOW DOWN AND ACCEPT MOMENTS OF KINDNESS FROM OTHERS T&Cs: Must be savoured	This coupon entitles you to: SPEND A MORNING READING IN BED T&Cs: Must be savoured	This coupon entitles you to: A MOVIE NIGHT AT HOME WITH SOME POPCORN T&Cs: Must be savoured	This coupon entitles you to: A CANDLE-LIT BATH T&Cs: Must be savoured
This coupon entitles you to: A MEAL WITH A FRIEND T&Cs: Must be savoured	This coupon entitles you to: READ A BOOK T&Cs: Must be savoured	This coupon entitles you to: SMELL THE ROSES T&Cs: Must be savoured	This coupon entitles you to: A TRIP TO A GALLERY OR MUSEUM T&Cs: Must be savoured

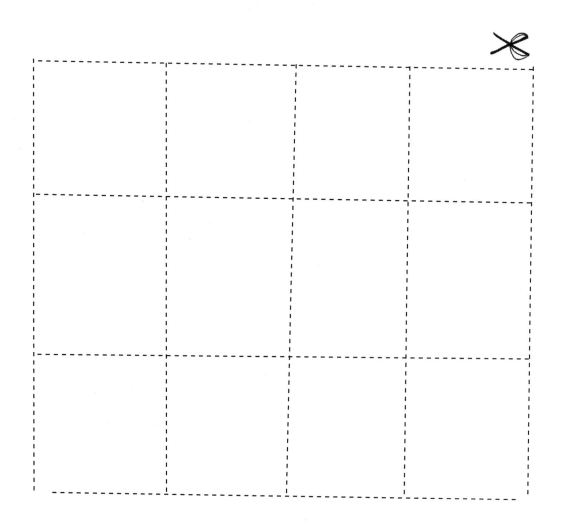

SINGING IN THE RAIN
54

This coupon entitles you to: TAKE AN AFTERNOON NAP T&Cs: Must be savoured	This coupon entitles you to: GIVE YOURSELF A HUG T&Cs: Must be savoured	This coupon entitles you to: A LUNCH BREAK IN THE PARK, LYING IN THE SUN T&Cs: Must be savoured	This coupon entitles you to: A HOMEMADE SMOOTHIE T&Cs: Must be savoured
This coupon entitles you to: T&Cs: Must be savoured	This coupon entitles you to: T&Cs: Must be savoured	This coupon entitles you to: T&Cs: Must be savoured	This coupon entitles you to: T&Cs: Must be savoured
This coupon entitles you to: T&Cs: Must be savoured	This coupon entitles you to: T&Cs: Must be savoured	This coupon entitles you to: T&Cs: Must be savoured	This coupon entitles you to: T&Cs: Must be savoured
This coupon entitles you to: T&Cs: Must be savoured	This coupon entitles you to: T&Cs: Must be savoured	This coupon entitles you to: T&Cs: Must be savoured	This coupon entitles you to: T&Cs: Must be savoured

12.

PLAYING LIKE A CHILD

It's deep winter as I write this. There's nothing like waking up to a sprinkling of icing-sugar snow to rouse the child in us. Which is how I felt momentarily when I drew the curtains and gasped at the silvery white blanket outside my window. Looking at the snow made me feel fun and playful, rather than serious and grown-up. I wanted to rush outside and make a snowman, just for the sake of making a snowman. But then I thought, 'Oh dear, how will I get to work? And will I be cold?'

Children see snow and cry 'Yay!' They run outside and enjoy the deliciousness of the snowflakes and icicles, playing with them, looking at the drifts in front of them, without all the analysis that quickly overtakes an adult mind. It can be a wonderful de-stressor to cultivate a reconnection with this sense of child-like, rather than childish, joy. And it is a shame we lose this ability as we supposedly grow up. So often children are wiser than us. They can convey important messages with breath-taking simplicity.

Compared to adults, children naturally have less developed cognitive skills – this is the thinking brain system that gives us the ability to regret the past and imagine the future. Instead, they enjoy the moment. By contrast, as we get older and more experienced, we can forget to live in the present.

As adults, we are often focused on results. Of course, reaching our goals does make us happy... but only temporarily. This phenomenon is called the hedonic treadmill, used to describe how we continuously raise the bar for what we need to feel content. By contrast, one of the joys of our childhood pastimes is that we did them just because they were fun, rather than because of anything they might lead to.

Remembering what absorbed us when we were children can be a good way of returning to this state.

Time to jump out of bed and make a snowman.

Your turn to remind yourself of what you loved as a child and reawaken that enjoyment of activities just for the sake of them:

1. Find a photo of yourself as a child and stick it in the space below.
Ideally, it would be of you doing an activity you used to enjoy.
If you can't find a photo, a sketch is fine.

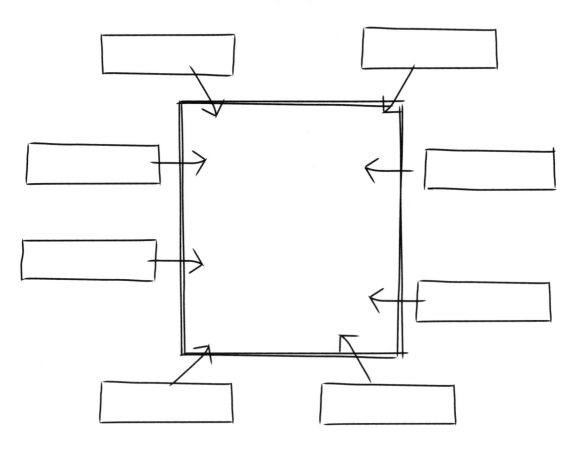

2. Remember what activities made you happy when you were little. You might consider what sports you enjoyed, whether you liked dressing up or acting, or playing imaginary games. Perhaps you enjoyed making things or drawing? Write the answers in some of the boxes around the picture opposite.

3. Underline those activities you might benefit from taking up again. You could consider an adult version of your childhood pleasures. So, if you wrote that you loved ballet classes as a child, this might translate into a dance class at your gym. If you loved dressing up, perhaps you could join an amateur acting society.

4. Are there any existing pastimes you could adapt into more playful activities by changing the way you do them or the way you think about them? It could be as simple as going for a bike ride with no destination in mind rather than cycling to work. Write these in the remaining empty boxes around your photo.

5. Enjoy all these activities whether they are new to your life or ones you've adapted to savour them as pleasures you can do for their own sake rather than for anything that will result from them.

The pleasure of reconnecting with your child-like side is summed up by this verse from Robert Louis Stevenson. His words are something you can turn to, whether it snows or not...

Happy hearts and happy faces,
Happy play in grassy places –
That was how, in ancient ages,
Children grew to kings and sages.

(13.)

CHANTING, GARGLING AND HUMMING

It has taken me a while to add this next exercise to my collection of practical steps to happiness, perhaps because I was put off by the gynaecological overtones of its name – vagal toning. But a few months ago I changed my tune (pun intended) when I learnt that Edward Bullmore, professor of psychiatry at Cambridge University, believes that mental disorders may have their root cause in the immune system and looks at inflammation as a key factor. Stimulating our vagus nerve at the back of our throats may help reduce this unhelpful inflammation.

This nerve is so called because it wanders to so many different places in the body, like a vagabond. It begins in the brain stem, and then passes through the back of the throat before branching out when it reaches our digestive system and even stretches to a tiny part of the external ear canal. It acts automatically, increasing our heart rate and blood pressure when we are under stress and relaxing them when the threat passes.

So far, studies have found that stimulating the vagus nerve can help reduce inflammation in those suffering from arthritis. Scientists are investigating whether vagus nerve stimulation will also prove an effective treatment for low mood. While we await more research, vagal toning is pleasant and soothing.

There are several ways to do this. One method is to buy a device a bit like a plastic pebble that pulses and thrums like a bass speaker and which is positioned over the nerve itself on your chest. The stimulation activates the vagus nerve by putting the brakes on the body's own stress response, which is why it feels so calming.

The audible vibration we create and experience when chanting, gargling or humming can also stimulate the vagus nerve. This could explain why chanting, and especially the 'om' sound are used in yoga and meditative practices.

Vagal toning may sound rather unsavoury, but I would be surprised if we didn't hear more about its efficacy in future. Om I go.

Your turn to stimulate your vagus nerve to induce calm:

1. To chant a long, low 'om':

● Place one hand on your heart and the other on your belly.

● Feel the vibration in your abdomen and chest too as you say 'om' as slowly as possible.

● Make sure the 'mmmmm' part of the om is the longest part of the chant.

2. Other ideas include:

● Gargling for a few seconds with water when you clean your teeth, making the lowest sound you can without straining.

● Humming or singing in the shower – you know you want to!

● Do some belly breathing – see page 14.

FIRST
APPRECIATION
PAUSE

Take a moment to congratulate yourself on getting this far, and pause to consider what you feel appreciative of

You are a quarter of the way through the book, and I hope you are finding these first 13 activities are relatively easy to incorporate in your life. You may even be feeling a bit calmer.

Now take a moment to stop, relax and congratulate yourself on getting this far. This is the first of four pauses throughout the book to stop and enjoy a pleasant thought. In contrast to my suggested activities, this is about thinking, not doing.

All you need do is sit comfortably, and then let your mind turn to something you appreciate about yourself, someone else or a recent positive experience. Your list could include anything from appreciating the hard work you've done in this book so far to a meal with friends, feeling the sun on your face, someone praising your work or having an understanding partner. Just take a few moments to ponder what you feel appreciative of and really enjoy that feeling.

Well done! Now it's back to the drawing board...

DEVELOPING YOUR VOICE

14.

MANAGING WORRY

I have traditionally been good at worrying. It's my specialist subject and has been ever since I was small. In fact, according to family history, some of my earliest sentences began, 'I am worried that...' – pronounced 'wor-rid.' As I grew up, I often felt like I was skating on thin ice: my mind would spin around and around, and each time the marks on the ice would get deeper, just like my worries. And of course, I could start worrying about worrying: would the ice crack altogether? And would I tumble into the freezing blue depths beneath the surface?

A key psychological shift occurred when I realised a few years ago that worrying didn't help. In fact, the energy it required took away from solving my problems. And the best first step to stop worrying was to make a list of my worries. This allowed me to see more clearly which were proper problems, and which were just minor concerns. Without a list, I was giving all worries equal weight. For example, the trivial matter of what to wear to a party would be vying for attention with a serious need to make sure I saw a doctor about a longstanding complaint.

I now choose a time each day when I make a date with my worries. It is best to do this first thing and get the process out of the way as early as possible. 'Good morning, worries!' I think to myself. 'This is your time! Your worry window! Here are your five minutes in the limelight!'

Putting things off is stressful. Not facing up to a challenging meeting or chat actually makes it worse as we dread what lies ahead. By contrast, if we get what is bothering us out of the way as soon as possible, we can enjoy the rest of our day.

I spend around five minutes writing down my list of worries. This offloads information onto the paper, freeing up my headspace. My brain can relax because it knows I am on to the worries. And here's the clever bit: when my worries pop up later in the day, they do not distract me because I know I have an allotted slot for dealing with them.

I divide my list into worries which are priorities, and those which are unimportant, as well noting things I can do something about. In doing so, I may discover practical information that may make the situation better. If I can do something, I record by each concern my action plan and when I will carry it out. And if I can't do anything, I know I need to accept that difficulty with gentleness and self-compassion, which may prove the tougher task.

So today my list of worries looks something like this, with my own notes-to-self jotted down after each worry, as shown in the exercise on page 68.

- My mum's chemotherapy treatment. (Priority. Nothing I can do to stop this. No action plan. Reminder to myself to be self-compassionate – of course I am worried about my mum: seeing a loved one suffer is hard.)

- I have an interview with a company first thing in the morning, which is my worst time of day. (Not a priority. Nothing I can do to change this. No action plan, just a need for acceptance. This is obviously not a serious problem in the same league as mum's chemotherapy. Of course these thoughts are there, you have a long history of being anxious first thing. But be gentle on yourself.)

- I was impatient and on the verge of being rude when asking for a piece of work from a colleague who I find challenging. (Not a priority. Yes, I can do something about this. Problem solving – stop and find a time to talk to her. Could I meet her in the middle, or compromise?)

- Managing to meet the deadline on my next article, which is today. (Priority. Yes, I can do something. Problem solving – extend the deadline or break this task down somehow?)

Accepting we can't change things, like my mother's cancer treatment, is hard. It feels like an angry, fiery knot of fury. Many have grappled with how best to do so. Some find the approach of the twelve-step Alcoholics Anonymous programme helpful. I like the serenity prayer: 'God grant me the serenity to accept the things I cannot change; the courage to change the things I can; and the wisdom to know the difference', as well the thirteenth-century Persian poem 'The Guesthouse' written by the mystic Rumi. The last lines are: 'Be grateful for whoever comes/ because each has been sent/ as a guide from beyond.' I also have found doing a loving kindness meditation, which combines slow breathing with a charitable statement, can make acceptance easier.

On a more optimistic note, have you noticed how often what you worry about never actually happens? In a few weeks' or months' time take a look at what you were worried about today. More often than not, what we thought would trouble us turns out to be tolerable, or just never happens. Late in life, Mark Twain reflected, 'I am an old man and have known a great many troubles, but most of them have never happened.'

Now it is your turn to re-arrange your overwhelming thoughts and reduce worrying time:

- Decide on a time each day, preferably in the morning, when you will note down your worries. Think of this as your worry window.

- On a piece of paper, draw a box at the top, as shown opposite, and write down all the worries you are facing.

- Go through the list. For each worry, decide if it is a priority or not. Focus on the priorities.

- Concentrating on priorities, decide if a worry is something you can act on. Spend a few minutes problem solving if you can. Then draw an Action plans box in which to write it down on your 'act on' list.

- If you can't do anything about a particular worry, put this in a 'can't act on' list. Acknowledge that those fiery knots of worry are a legitimate part of your mental landscape.

- Try a meditation. Breathe in and out calmly, then make one of the following statements. Then breathe in and out again before you make another statement.

May I be safe from harm
May I be happy just as I am
May I be peaceful with
whatever is happening

- Resolve to focus on where you can make a difference rather than dwelling on things you can't change. Your thought process might look something like the diagram opposite:

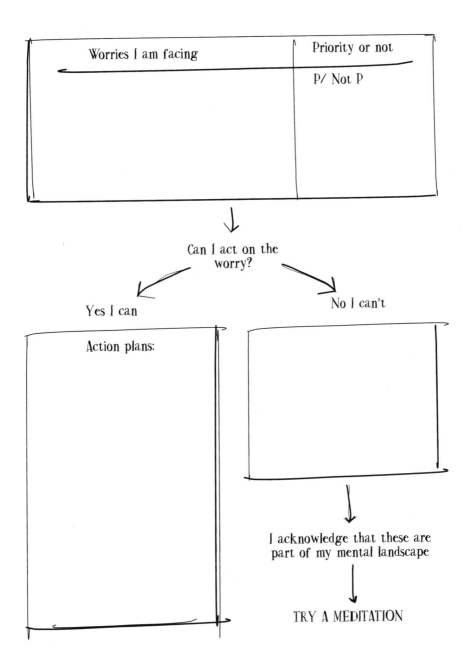

Worries I am facing	Priority or not
	P/ Not P

Can I act on the worry?

Yes I can   No I can't

Action plans:

I acknowledge that these are
part of my mental landscape

TRY A MEDITATION

(15.)

BEING KIND TO OTHERS

This week I was rushing for a train, fumbling for my ticket at the bottom of my bag. I was aware of the queue forming behind me and was feeling hot and sweaty. (You'll know by now that I'm a nervous traveller.) Then the ticket officer opened the gate for me, letting me through with a wave. As I settled into my grey seat, I pondered random acts of kindness from people we have never met, and the power of a stranger's care.

Often it is a case of pausing to appreciate the person who has reached out as just that – a person rather than someone merely performing a function. This could be my ticket officer this week, or the individual who picks up something you have dropped, or the stranger who holds the lift for you. Just notice and receive their kindness.

In turn, we can be kind to those who cross our path by chance. We live in a technological age where being on our phones makes it easy to avoid interaction. But even a gentle text or call to say 'Are you okay?' can change someone's day. This requires us to become more attentive to how we might lighten someone's load: to identify that person struggling with their bags in a shop, and offer to help carry them.

It can be hard to reach out to others, especially if you are not feeling strong. If this is the case, remember when you have been in need of a helping hand. You could start thinking about the little 'imperfect' quirks you have and try to see yourself through the eyes of someone else. Everyone has their oddities. Also remind yourself of our common humanity. We all suffer. That's my default thought if I am feeling less than saintly towards others, such as my immediate neighbours when I'm stuck on a crowded Tube.

You might find it helpful to set an intention first thing in the morning to behave in this way. Then notice if your own small, heart-warming acts throughout the day promote the same impulse in others. Social scientists call it the 'three-degree rule'. Each time we influence someone, they in turn influence someone else, who in turn influences a third person.

The size of the gesture doesn't matter. I love the story of a child and a man on a beach, based on a tale by the late US anthropologist, Loren Eiseley, called *The Star Thrower*. A man is walking down a long beach, along which there are thousands of starfish carried ashore by the waves. The starfish will soon die unless returned to the water. The man spots a child progressing along the shoreline, throwing the starfish back into the water one by one. The man tells the child it is a useless thing to do: there are so many stranded starfish; throwing one or two back in will make no difference. The child looks at him, picks up another starfish, and throws it into the sea. 'Well, it made a difference to that one,' he says.

Being compassionate towards an individual starfish or anyone else clearly benefits them. But we know that it has a positive effect on us too. Altruism isn't entirely selfless. When you are kind to others in distress a feel-good hormone known as endorphins is released. This is sometimes known as a 'helper's high'. Perhaps I should lose my ticket more often...

P.S. As well as responding to random opportunities to be kind, you might want to consider doing some volunteering or charity work. Research suggests that volunteers tend to live longer and have lower blood pressure than non-volunteers.

If this feels overwhelming, you could consider helping out on an ad hoc basis when you feel up to it, or over Christmas for example. My own best days of the week are when I volunteer at our local prison or work for the various mental health charities with which I am involved. It gives me the warmest feeling when I remember some of the nice things people have said about my work. I don't know if anything else makes me as satisfied or boosts my mood more.

Your turn to help others:

Read through the first three instructions below. Then close your eyes and think about each scenario in turn.

1. First, to put yourself in the right mood to reach out to others you don't know, bring to mind the suffering of someone who is important to you. Let this feeling of compassion fill your mind. Spend a minute or so thinking about someone who has suffered.

2. Extend that feeling to others around you, with a willingness to help and perform random acts of kindness to those you have never met in the future. Spend a minute or so thinking about these acts in the future.

3. You might also like to cast your thoughts back over all those strangers who have helped you through your life till now, from a teacher at school to an employer at work or a grandparent who looked after you. Spend a minute or so thinking about those in the past who have helped you.

4. As you pass your day, build in time to react to others in a kindly way, if natural moments arise when it's appropriate to do so. Become more observant of what people are trying to achieve. Can you help them achieve it? This is about responding to others. Here are some ideas that you might include – circle those that appeal to you.

• Spend a few minutes talking to a stranger in a café or the canteen.
• Pay attention to what someone is saying when they talk to you. Listen to understand and not to reply.
• Give up your seat for someone on the train.
• Buy lunch for a homeless person.
• Allow someone to go in ahead of you in the queue.
• Pay a compliment.

5. To remind you how this kind of behaviour can also benefit you, at the end of the week jot down what you did and how it made you feel on a scale of 1-10 in the following table.

DAY	Act of kindness to someone else	How did it make you feel? (choose a number between 1-10)

(16.)

FINDING PERSPECTIVE

Walking home through a rough bit of land in the park at dusk, I stepped on what I thought was solid ground. It turned out to be a hole hidden beneath the high yellowing grass. I fell heavily, hurting my leg. I had bruised and cut my thigh, which was nicely scarlet and beginning to swell. I felt myself spiral into fear. I imagined the injury was serious, perhaps even the leg was broken, and I would need time in hospital. I would miss important meetings, time with my sick mum, and I would fall into an abyss of worry. Very soon I imagined my leg was going to be chopped off altogether.

It is surprising how our clever and complex brains can build lengthy narratives within seconds in this way, especially if, like me, you are practised in absolutist, short-cut thinking. This thinking habit is known as catastrophising, when our mind is our own worst enemy and we make mountains out of molehills. We need to realise that dark thoughts aren't helpful. There are two ways of doing this. The first is to regain a sense of perspective, and then once you have done so, to distract yourself.

Regaining perspective begins with observing our language when we catastrophise. So instead of telling myself, 'I am terrified I will lose the use of my leg,' I might say, 'I am slightly worried.' Instead of 'My leg is in agony,' 'My leg hurts a bit.'

Then arrange your thoughts in an orderly way. First, allow the catastrophic thoughts to reach a worst-case scenario (the worst case is my leg doesn't work ever again). Then imagine the best-case scenario, building your thoughts incrementally (the best case is my leg stops hurting). And finally, think of the most likely scenario, (the most likely case is my leg is gently strained, it will stop hurting soon, and I will see a doctor shortly).

The idea is that the best-case scenario thinking takes the edge off the fight-or-flight emotion enough to enable us to plan, using the neocortex. It is also based on the finding that once catastrophising starts, it is very difficult to stop. By contrast, thinking about the most likely scenario gives you back some control as you can imagine what you might do about the situation (in this case, organise to see a doctor).

A reality check can be helpful for building this kind of perspective. Firstly, consider how the episode might look to you in the future, particularly compared to the fate of others who may be in far trickier and more challenging situations. You could imagine how it might look in ten minutes time, ten months time, or ten years time. Second, you could consider how what has happened will look to others. Then reassure yourself that, mostly, they are too concerned about their own worries to dwell on what is happening to you.

Finally, catastrophic thoughts are always worse at night. Avoid challenging topics past 8 p.m. I agreed this with my husband recently: we reduced the number of times we argued by not discussing sensitive topics past this cut-off point, when we are usually both knackered.

Once I've regained some perspective by following these steps, there is often a pause until the future is clearer. This is where my second method becomes relevant. We need to distract ourselves by focusing on a specific task – which today means origami. Under pressure, fold.

It turns out that paper folding has been recommended by doctors as a useful activity to divert patients on hospital wards. In the past my efforts to create a crane in full flight looked more like a squashed paper bag. But there is no doubt that the concentration required fixes me in the moment and stops me worrying about the future. Moving my eyes back and forth from the instructions to the paper in my hand means I stop panicking about my leg.

Studies suggest an unfocused mind is almost always less happy than a mind that is paying attention to what it's doing. Our minds tend to drift to negative thoughts when unfocused, as they involve unresolved conflicts. The brain hates unresolved conflicts and is drawn to try and sort them out. A diversion, such as origami or reading a book, can give our brains a break, after which we can return to the issue with a new perspective. Then mountains really do become molehills and sore legs stop hurting quite so much too.

Your turn to find perspective and then ground yourself with a spot of origami:

To regain perspective, use moderate language while you imagine:

1. What is the worst-case scenario?

2. What is the best-case scenario?

3. What is the most likely scenario?

4. In the most likely scenario, what can you control?

5. What can you change?

6. When are you going to change it?

7. Compare your fate to that of others.

8. Consider how the episode will look in the future – in one week? One month? One year?

To distract yourself:

Take a piece of blank paper and follow the instructions opposite to make an origami boat.

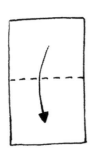

a) Fold in half

b) Fold in half again and unfold

c) Fold to the centre

d) Fold the overlapping strip upwards

e) Fold the corners backwards. Turn over

f) Fold the strip upwards

g) Open

h) Fold triangle upwards. Repeat behind

i) Open (same as step g)

j) Take the upper corners and stretch out

l) Finished boat

17.

COLOURING

Colouring books first came into my life when I needed an activity that I could do alongside a ten-year-old nephew who needed entertaining in the holidays as he was convalscing. We both wanted something that didn't involve being on our phones.

I wanted a simple design to ease us into the world of colouring. So we began by colouring in a circle filled with basic geometric designs, sometimes known as a mandala after the Sanskrit word for circle. The mandala image was good for beginners like us. I knew we would have a chance of finishing the picture, as it wasn't too challenging. We decided we would only use five or six colours, so as not to be flummoxed by too many choices. We also used felt-tip pens rather than coloured pencils. Pencils would have allowed us to create even more colours by mixing two shades together. We wanted less choice, not more, as too many decisions at this stage of our colouring career would have been stressful.

Conversation flowed easily as we sat side by side in a happy bubble of shared endeavour. The simple repetitive action of shading was soothing. I didn't have to be creative; I just had to colour in someone else's design. There were literal boundaries as to what was being asked of me. We ended up with something tangible: a picture. I think most of all I liked the physicality of the action. Stress that had been building up seemed to flow down my arm, through the felt-tip pen, to be released onto the paper in technicolor.

It was a way for me to be present and to notice my mind wandering from the page and back. Over time, my nephew relaxed too.

I graduated from completing easy designs like the one I did with my nephew to colouring in images, which were more challenging as they were surrounded by blank space. These required me to use my imagination by drawing something extra. I felt less daunted when I thought of it as doodling rather than drawing. You may find your own artistic temperament is similarly stimulated. Colouring may prove a gateway to a drawing or pottery class where your own creativity can flourish. Or just colour for calm, nephews not required.

Your turn to use colouring in to ground yourself:

1. If possible, use felt-tip pens rather than pencils to colour the mandala on the next page. But it is up to you! If you have no felt tips to hand, make use of what you do have.

2. If you do use colours, restrict your colour palette to three or four colours, from the same spectrum.

3. Progress to colouring in the second more complex mandala. Use all the colours you have, and include shading to add even more texture and interest to your colour palette.

4. Create some extra detail of your own in the blank space that surrounds the mandala. You might add in some more circular shapes, or jagged shapes as a contrast. It is up to you.

5. Colour in those extra details too.

SINGING IN THE RAIN
80

(18.)

BEING HAPPY NOT PERFECT

I have spent much of the morning trying to find the right sentence with which to start an article. I am playing with the phrase 'it is a truth universally acknowledged', but I don't like borrowing from Jane Austen. I am aware it's a clichéd approach, yet I can't find an alternative. The harder I try to perfect my sentence, the worse it reads. I know I must stop soon or I will trip over a hidden rabbit hole I know only too well – that of being a perfectionist.

Feeling we must be perfect is a growing problem in our digital age: comparing our humdrum existence with the shiny lives of celebrities makes us feel that anything less than perfect is not good enough. Yet often it is those who shine most brightly and seem to have supposedly perfect lives who actually find life the hardest. The brighter the light, the darker the shadow. One study even links some types of perfectionism to increased rates of suicide.

In some cases, setting exacting standards can be appropriate – if you are a surgeon or a pilot, for example. But in my own less exacting life it is easy to apply perfectionist standards when they are not needed, or are inappropriate or even damaging. In the past, I have set myself overly high ideals and imagined there is no middle way between succeeding and failing: a frightening prospect. And because my standards were too demanding, I have often felt a failure, as naturally I have not always met those standards. I have concentrated on what has gone wrong, with little compassion for myself, rather than remembering what has gone right. What could be less motivating than focusing on our blunders?

How then to change? Start by thinking of someone you admire. Now consider. Did they ever fluff anything? Of course they did! Then, recognise perfectionism is often linked to a black-and-white thinking approach, which I write about in *Flexible thinking* on page 218. I am either a brilliant writer or a dreadful clichéd hack. Of course neither are true. Replace this approach with a gentler, more realistic narrative. Note what you have achieved rather than what you have failed to do. And remind yourself that by cracking on, over time your writing will improve (you hope).

I like the story of a ceramics teacher who divided his pupils into two groups. One group was asked to make as many pots as they could, and the other group to make one perfect pot. In the end, the group who focused on quantity rather than quality made the best pots. Their pots were smoother, with less bumps and a more pleasing shape, even though the students produced more, and worked more quickly. Why? Because those who made more pots were trying, failing and learning. Those who were trying for the perfect pot didn't take any risks for fear of failure, which is why their skills didn't improve. Fail more, but master more too.

As few of us have access to a kiln, I have adapted this idea and there is a flower drawing exercise on the next page. It is not about being brilliant and including every last floral detail. It is about giving something a go.

Imperfect action is better than perfect inaction. You could develop this idea by deliberately trying to do something less well, just to see what happens. Try giving yourself a time frame, as procrastination and perfectionism are linked. It's harder to stay a perfectionist when you have a set time period in which to complete a task, which is not the same as an invitation to rush.

When you have finished your drawings, ask someone else about the images. Sometimes our anxiety about perfectionism is because we worry about what others will think, which holds us back. Yet in reality, others tend not to expect the level of detail or skill we feel we need to provide. Imagining their criticism demotivates us. That is a truth that's universally acknowledged.

See also *Quitting comparing* on page 234 and *Challenging mind writing* on page 210.

Your turn to be less of a perfectionist:

1. Get some coloured pens out.

2. In the first box below, draw a picture of one flower and take as long as you like.

3. In the second box, draw a field full of flowers and set a timer for ten minutes.

4. Ask someone else which picture they prefer.

5. And ask yourself which flowers you had more fun drawing. (Hint: it should be the second!)

(19.)

SOCIALISING AND FRIENDSHIPS

There's a joy to voluntary solitude when we happily spend time with ourselves. No one put it better than the poet, William Wordsworth:

When from our better selves we have too long been parted by the hurrying world, and droop. Sick of its business, of its pleasures tired, how gracious, how benign is Solitude.

This feels quite different to loneliness, when we crave connection with others. Two thousand years ago, Aristotle pointed out that man is a social animal, and now we have research that shows how loneliness affects our wellbeing: it can lead to premature mortality, just like obesity or smoking.

Whether it's because of the rise of the online world, which is itself a sign of the longing we have for connection, or the breakdown of family relationships, or overwork, or lack of time, the reality is that too many of us feel isolated. We need and want to connect more with others. Feeling connected fosters better physical health and a longer life: some studies show that being with others is as effective as exercise in promoting good health. Try closing your eyes and remembering when you were last happy: I suspect your memory will include other people.

I think about connecting with others in two ways. First there's socialising. I think of this as everyday superficial social activity, when we make small talk with all those whom we randomly encounter, or see over the course of our day, be it at work or at a yoga class. These are people we don't know well, and may or may not see again. Secondly, there is spending time with more intimate friends. Both are important for our wellbeing.

Recent research shows the first kind of light-touch socialising can boost our mood. One simple idea is to formalise tea breaks at work, in the way that we used to do in the past when famously all of England stopped at 4 p.m. for a cuppa. The Swedes down tools and pick up a mug twice a day for communal get-togethers known as 'fika'.

So if making new friends sounds daunting, a more helpful approach may be just to interact more with others in this casual way. Even just a 'good morning' or a 'thank you' can make you feel more connected. This kind of informal socialising can lead to closer friendships. It's valuable even if it doesn't.

Second, there's connecting more profoundly, and increasing our opportunities for deeper friendships. Ironically, one way to feel closer to others is to enjoy conversations that move beyond the superficial and to admit to our vulnerability about feeling lonely. Move on from small talk and take a bit longer to ask what someone did at his or her weekend. Listen to their answer and ask a follow-up question before offering an insight into your own state of mind. Paying attention is the most basic kind of love. We all know how isolated we can feel even in a crowded room if that deeper connection is not there. If someone sympathetic asks you how you are, it is okay to be honest and say you feel low.

Another way of fostering this deeper connection with others is to do something new, rather than just meeting on a Friday night for a drink. Recently I joined some friends for a guided tour of an exhibition at a gallery. We joked and chatted more in that hour gawping at the pictures than in years of other get-togethers. Our tongues were loosened as the social pressure was off: it was less of a social outing, more of an event we just happened to be doing together. Even better, make these expedi-

tions a regular commitment. I know I am more likely to stick to a social engagement when it's regular, when I have paid for it, and when I feel I am letting others down if I don't go.

You may need to ponder what type of gatherings you most enjoy for more intimate relationships. I know one person who was in danger of feeling isolated, as he had ceased to enjoy socialising with the large groups he had previously spent time with. These occasions made him feel bad, as if there was something wrong with him and he stopped going out as much. But his social life changed when he realised that he wasn't the problem: it was the scale of the events. He likes small groups of friends, five or six at the most, and enjoys meeting for intimate suppers when they cook together.

Whether you look at the English word 'companion', the Spanish word 'compañero' or the French 'copain', they all originate from the Latin 'com' and 'panis', meaning 'with whom one shares bread'. Food nurtures our friendship as much as our bodies, and eating together is probably the one social thing we could aspire to do more frequently. Research suggests eating alone is associated with unhappiness, something which would have not surprised the Ancient Greek philosopher Epicurus, who said, 'Consider carefully whom you eat or drink with rather than what you eat or drink; for feeding without a friend is the life of a lion or a wolf'.

Finally, feeling part of a neighbourhood can foster regular interaction and in time a feeling of friendship. Meik Wiking, from the Happiness Research Institute in Copenhagen, cites the Dutch proverb that it's better to have a close neighbour than a distant friend. He advises dropping a sign-up sheet through the letterboxes on your street or in your building to create a list in case of burst pipes or other emergencies, which in turn can open up more exciting conversations on other topics. We did actually do this in the last street we lived in and it was eye-opening how much friendlier we all became. Wiking's other ideas include creating a book-lending cupboard in your front garden on the take-one-leave-one principle or making a point of sitting on your porch or front garden if you have one.

I know, it does all sound a bit self-conscious, and you might prefer to start by smiling more at your neighbours and asking the odd question about their day. But if it's good enough for the Danes, who routinely come top of those happiness surveys, then it's good enough for me.

See also *Eating for calm and focus* on page 36.

Your turn to plan how you will engage more with others:

Random socialising – tick the options you might try:

- Chatting to the postman or shopkeeper
- Going to a yoga or exercise class
- Taking part in a 'Borrow my Dog' scheme
- Formalising tea breaks at work

Making deeper friendships:

Plan an outing with others doing something you have never done together before or going to a place you have never been before as a group. You might consider:

- Visiting a museum
- Going to a drawing class
- Going on a picnic
- Playing a board game or football or basketball

Make a list of social events you will commit to here:

....

....

....

Organise one date to eat a meal with a companion

Building a community:

Create a questionnaire for your street. Alongside asking for names, you could plant the seeds of a community by asking:

- How long have you lived here?
- Do you have any recommendations about the area you would like to share?
- Or local tradesmen or shops you would like to recommend?
- Or anything you are searching for that someone else might be able to help you with? A babysitter or a computer whizz?

(20.)

EMBEDDING NEW HABITS

Well done! You are nearly halfway through the book, and I hope you are not feeling overwhelmed by all the ideas I have suggested so far. It would be great if you have managed to include any of these practical steps at all in your life. You may be struggling to stick to them. Our reward-seeking limbic brains (for more on brains see my website: rachel-kelly.net) naturally seek out quick existing pleasurable hits rather than embracing new habits that might initially seem like hard work (which is why children find it difficult to start their homework). Here's what helps keep me on track.

First, frame your habits in terms of what you want to add to your life, or do more of, or become, not on what you would like to be rid of or stop. If we frame habits as things we mustn't do, like 'I must not stay up late', the mind has a way of focusing on the forbidden. So the habit you wish to adopt is to get up earlier. Equally, instead of saying 'I will be less of a perfectionist', you could decide that 'I will become gentler on myself'. You can extend this idea to identifying with the person you will become: an early riser

and a more forgiving person.

Next, jot down lots of activities you wish to adopt. This kind of brainstorming reassures me that I have not forgotten anything. I then slim down my list to just two or three (although I know I can always come back to the longer version). Research suggests it is best to focus on fewer new habits, with each one having what researchers call an 'implementation plan'.

When a habit-change seems too big and you don't know where to begin, it is easy to feel frightened and give up. To avoid this, break down your two or three aims into even smaller steps – your implementation plan. Then flesh this out in a bit more detail. When do you plan to start on your new habit? Is there a location in whichyou might do this? Is there anything you need to put in place to make your new behaviour more likely?

So, if your aim was to move more, you could start straight away; you could do so on your journey to and from work; you could buy a pair of trainers. This detailed planning makes it more likely you will progress towards your new habit, because it feels more achievable and tangible and, once underway, things are more likely to continue and flow.

Going with the flow is much easier than using finite willpower. So put exercise and social commitments in your calendar, if that's your new approach, weeks ahead. If you set up regular times in this way, it's much easier than organising meet-ups one-by-one.

Research suggests that some of our habits are triggered by specific contexts rather than our intentions, and we can make those contexts easier for ourselves.

Try involving others in your commitment. I am more consistent when I make public promises, (though I know from my workshops and feedback that the opposite is true for others). So you could try telling a friend or colleague your two or three targets, and ask that they do the same to you and formalise this process by writing commitment cards to each other – the exercise shows you how. Then, say, a month later, meet up and see how you are both progressing. I was so interested to hear how a friend was getting along, and know this interest motivated her, too. And she did the same for me.

Start on the first small step. Action leads to motivation, not the other way round. Good luck!

Your turn to choose your aims and stick to your new habits:

---

1. Here are some activities described in the book so far. Choose three of them that align well with your own aims.

1. Belly breathing
2. Rising early
3. Dressing well
4. Smiling and laughing
5. Visualising
6. Moving
7. Eating for calm
8. Sitting and standing
9. Relaxing physically
10. Enjoying simple pleasures
11. Playing like a child
12. Chanting, gargling and humming
13. Managing worry
14. Being kind to others
15. Finding perspective
16. Colouring
17. Reflecting on your roots

Activity 1
is...

Activity 2
is...

Activity 3
is...

2. Break each of these three new activities into a few achievable steps, and record them in the stepping stones opposite. Ask yourself these questions to guide you.

● When and where will you start?

● Is there anything you need to put in place to make your aim more likely?

● Can you set a timeframe in which you will achieve your aim? – Is it a sensible time in your life to take on this aim?

Fill in the steps below for your action plan:

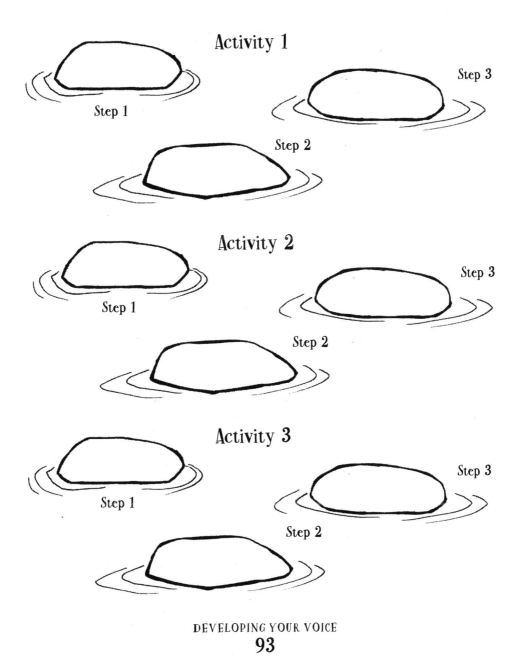

Activity 1

Step 1

Step 2

Step 3

Activity 2

Step 1

Step 2

Step 3

Activity 3

Step 1

Step 2

Step 3

3 Write a commitment card to someone else

● Find someone to be your commitment buddy. If you prefer, you can make a promise to yourself.

● Fill in the card below.

● Get someone else to sign and witness it if you are working with a buddy, or sign it yourself if not.

● Do the same for someone else if you are working as a pair.

Name   Date:

I commit to:

1.

2.

3.

Signed..

Witnessed..

(21.)

WRITING A THANK YOU LETTER

I have always enjoyed the rituals that surround letter writing, from the sealing of the envelope to the attaching of the stamp and the trip to a scarlet pillar-box. There's also a great pleasure to be had in receiving a proper handwritten message as the post falls through the letterbox with an intriguing clunk.

There are few nicer letters to write than ones that express gratitude to someone for the role they have played in our life. As I scribble away, I put aside my own worries and focus instead on what I'm thankful for. Anecdotal evidence collected about people in a nursing home found that one common regret among the dying is the wish that they had had the courage to express their feelings; a second is people wishing they had stayed in touch more with friends. Sending a letter saying why you care about someone combines both objectives.

Ideally, write by hand. This can feel odd in the digital age, but as we established at the start of this workbook, there is something to be said for it. For one thing, a handwritten letter can't be rushed.

It's a chance to examine your emotional connection with someone in more depth. I wrote my first appreciation letter to my godmother several years ago. It was difficult to write, as we tend not to be overly gushing in my family. Yet she was delighted. A few years later, my godmother's son told me my letter was one of the items from home she asked to be brought to her hospital bedside when she fell ill.

I have found one useful question is to ask how this other person has made me feel and what they have done to supppot me. As the poet Maya Angelou said, you will forget what someone did, but not how they made you feel. When I wrote to my godmother, I remembered how she makes me feel special and cherished because she still remembers my birthday with a card.

A second useful question to answer in the letter is what exactly you wish to celebrate about that person. I have given you some prompts on the next page.

Finally, make sure you say you are not expecting a response. The letter is not about you, it's about them, and some recipients may worry that they have to answer back. They don't.

Your turn to give time and thought to those you appreciate:

Use the prompts below to write your own appreciation letter. Think of a person who is very special to you. Who is the first person that comes to mind?

Dear ....

I wanted to say thank you for being my friend / supporter / colleague / ....

over the years. Some of the things you have done for me, or with me have included ....

....

These have made me feel ....

The qualities and strengths I most value you for are ....

....

The achievements of yours that I most admire include ....

....

I'm not expecting a response. Just know that I appreciate you.

Love,

....

(22.)

LISTENING TO MUSIC

Like most of us, I have a mad collection of songs and music in my head, everything from the tub-thumping hymn 'Jerusalem' to arias from Mozart's operas to the lyrical love songs of Dido with a bit of Jack Johnson thrown in. This eclectic mix reflects my own muddled musical tastes, particularly what I enjoyed as a teenager. But more recently, I have put in the effort to be more strategic about what I listen to and when. Playlists arranged by mood have become key parts of my happiness toolkit.

To relax, classical music is best. Scientists examined which kind of music most effectively reduced blood pressure after a stressful event. Some people were played Pachelbel's *Canon* and Vivaldi's *The Four Seasons: Spring*; others were played jazz and pop. Those who listened to the classical music relaxed more quickly, and their blood pressure dropped back to the normal level in less time.

To cheer us up, we need music to be funky, but not too funky. We respond best to groove music, a type of composition that isn't just a simple monotonous beat like a metronome but has an element of unpredictability: what is known as syncopation where the beat is displaced. But equally, we don't want our music to be too chaotic and unpredictable. Music like free jazz, for example, can be off-putting for some and doesn't make us want to dance with joy. Much modern pop music by contrast falls somewhere within the right range, where the syncopation is mid-way between predictable and chaotic. So too do the hits from many musicals. This kind of music elicits the most pleasure from us, and makes us want to dance.

Finally, music can make exercising more fun. I know I find music and exercise an effective pairing, almost as if music was a type of legal performance-enhancing drug, as one researcher put it. My own ability to endure going on a run is amplified by listening to a song like 'One Day More' from *Les Misérables*, with its complex melody and an energy that builds as the song progresses. It reminds me of the power of the performance when I saw the musical.

Within these guidelines, I've found that the songs I heard when I was a teenager have a more powerful effect on me than many others. While music lights a spark of neural activity in all of us, in the young the spark turns into a fireworks show. Between the ages of 12 and 22, our brains undergo rapid neurological development, and our memories are laden with heightened emotion, thanks to all those pubertal growth hormones. These hormones tell us that everything is important in this phase of our lives, including the songs we listen to.

I now have relaxing, cheerful and motivational playlists that make these feelings surface. I also use these playlists as triggers to reset my thoughts and moods if I have succumbed to negative thinking: music is an effective mood-changer as well as mood-booster. Even more so when we are belting a song out with others. Studies show that cortisol decreases when we sing. Auditioning for a choir is next on my list. But judging by my children's current response to my warblings, I think it unlikely anyone will sign me up anytime soon.

Your turn to create your own playlists for different moods:

Think about music that could fit into the playlists opposite, be they for relaxation, cheering yourself up or motivation. This process will probably take longer than a week but see how far you get in the next seven days. Then fill in your top ten mood-enhancing songs on the chart opposite.

When you have made your playlists, notice how different it makes you feel when you listen to songs with your whole being and when you pay attention to the lyrics. While the playlists are for you, listen to your music with others present when you can – and sing along, too.

Playlist for relaxation	Playlist for cheering up	Playlist for motivation
Look for: Slow beats per minute Regular rhythm Low pitch Tranquil melodies	Look for: Less regular beat Element of unpredictability in notes Happy memories and connotations	Look for: High number of beats per minute Positive lyrics Major keys

(23.)

TRAVELLING TO A JOYFUL PLACE

After all the exercises so far, you may be thinking it's time for a holiday. I still read the travel sections in the newspapers – old habits die hard after an earlier career as a journalist – and I don't feel self-indulgent when I do so. Some of the most productive people I know plan their time off with the same seriousness they bring to their work. Right now I do not want to travel far from home as my mother is unwell, but there's much to be said for imagining a future adventure.

In my mind, I'm in Spain, at the seaside, dreaming of all the markets I will visit, all the sun-ripened tomatoes that I will eat and all the dips in the Mediterranean that I will take. It turns out that water works a particular magic: pictures of nature that feature water make viewers more positive than pictures that feature only green landscapes. Sure enough, I feel my shoulders drop and my jaw relax if I think of the sea, as if I had already pulled the ripcord and parachuted out of my normal life. This kind of anticipatory pleasure can boost our mood as much as actually taking a trip away. Studies confirm the value of dreaming of a holiday, or what they describe as 'pre-trip happiness'.

I prefer travelling in a group, though I know others who relish the challenge and enjoy the freedom of being a solo traveller. If you are more like me, but can't find anyone to travel with, you might consider the many online sites that put like-minded travellers in touch.

Then there is the actual trip away, which of course is always a bit different from the fantasy we imagine ahead. This is the slight danger after all that anticipation – sometimes on arrival expectations are out of line with reality. You may need to take a moment consciously to accept how things are rather than how you think they should be. Throughout your trip, be attentive to the joys of the experience. Write postcards, however old-fashioned that seems. Use the moment to reflect on what you are enjoying. Not only will the recipient appreciate what you write in this digital age, but the exercise will also help you focus on what is special about being away. In addition, collect small mementoes, pictures and postcards to bring home.

Finally, make the most of your holiday memories – as long as you really did relax! Visualise where you went as a calming space to return to, a happy place where you felt comforted, safe and peaceful. You could intensify this process by using a souvenir from your holiday to help you recall it: perhaps a speckled stone you found on a beach. Remembering a particularly tranquil spot will reawaken those feelings in your mind.

All well and good, if you are able to travel. What if you are not? One reader shared her own peaceful place. 'I sit early in the morning in my tiny courtyard garden, quiet, with a coffee and next door's cat comes to sit with me. That's my happy place.' Right now, that feels just right for me too.

See also *Visualising* on page 29.

Your turn to bring your joyful place back to life:

Complete the page opposite to remind you of your happy place.
It could be after you come back from a peaceful break. Do this by:

- Recording the effect of your happy place on all your senses: sight, sound, taste, smell and touch.

- Noting down or drawing or doodling how the happy place makes you feel.

- Sticking in mementos and souvenirs of that special place.

What do you smell?

What do you see? The people around you? The landscape?

My happy place

Stick a souvenir here from your happy place, for example a picture, a train ticket or a postcard

Is there a way you feel when you visit your happy place?

What can you hear?

(24.)

CREATING SPACE FOR NEGATIVE FEELINGS

One stereotype is that women find it hard to acknowledge their anger, while men find it hard to accept their vulnerability. A broad generalisation for sure, but I've found it often to be true.

Both sexes can benefit from talking about and acknowledging such difficult feelings. The poet Robert Frost expressed it well: 'The best way out is always through.' The problem is that emotions can feel scary. We can diminish them by saying words like 'just' in phrases like 'I am just a bit annoyed' when in reality we are hopping furious. But we feel guilty about having negative feelings at all. And studies suggest those who feel bad about having dark thoughts have higher levels of depression and anxiety and lower levels of life satisfaction. So we do well to make friends with our emotions instead.

One way to do this is to investigate our difficult feelings. Because the alternative is often worse. If we suppress our emotions, we may turn to dangerous numbing behaviours such as drinking alcohol or eating too much food. In addition, shutting out our difficult feelings can lead to people failing to recognise our needs. Finally, when we hoard our feelings for too long, they tend to erupt, inappropriately.

How then can we become friendlier to our darker passions? My first method is to chat about my negative feeling with someone else. This person might be a psychotherapist, if you are lucky and able to afford one, or it could be your partner or great friend. Dark sentiments feel less shameful when we air them.

If discussing your negative feelings with someone else isn't something you feel comfortable doing, you might like to name an emotion aloud to yourself. A security announcement at some stations urges us to report anything unusual, with the slogan 'See it. Say it. Sorted'. I used to find it irritating until I saw how I could use the same approach with difficult feelings – see them, say them, sort them.

Or try writing down your distressing emotion, look back at what you wrote the next day, and I'd be surprised if that strong emotion hasn't diminished. You could even decide on one emotion you wish to observe during the course of the week – a 'feeling of the week' – to which you become attentive, and allow yourself to sit with it rather than to deny its presence.

Another idea is to imagine the emotion as a person. Tell them how you intend to manage your relationship with them by writing an actual letter. You might give them a colour, or describe them as an animal, or give them a name: Andy for Anxiety or Fred for Fear, with no disrespect intended to any Andys or Freds who might be reading this.

Exploring our darker emotions allows for deeper reflection. We realise that we can often feel more than one thing at the same time: when we say things not just in anger but in sorrow too; or when fear, for example, manifests itself as anger. Another approach is to give our older, more emotional mind a chance to meet our newer, analytical cognitive mind. Discussion between the two allows a space to open up around the feeling. We are stepping back from the feeling and becoming an observer.

You can help this distancing process by imagining that a difficult feeling doesn't belong to you: they are like clouds drifting past and never last forever – see also *Visualising* on page 29. Everything passes. In addition, try saying 'I feel sad at the moment' rather than 'I am sad.' This simple linguistic change helps, as it suggests a temporary rather than a permanent state of gloom. You can acknowledge the difficult emotion without catastrophising. Counter-intuitively, the phrase makes the feeling less overwhelming by recognising its importance.

The final challenge is to see if you can find anything positive in the negative emotion you are experiencing. It is not the emotion itself but what you do with it that matters. But that's for another week.

Your turn to investigate difficult feelings and to allow them some space rather than reacting to them:

Decide on a 'feeling of the week'. This week, become aware of that feeling in yourself, or indeed, in others.

● Which feeling will you choose?

Anger / Fear / Sadness

● Discuss your feelings with a supportive colleague, friend or professional: you might find going for a walk is the best time to do this.

● Write a letter to your difficult feeling instead.

● Use the prompts on the opposite page to get you started.

Dear.................................

I imagine you as a shape which looks like .... and feels like...................

.......................I see you as the colour .... I can also imagine you as an animal

such as a .... I give you the name...

I have noticed you tend to appear in my life at times when ....

....

I can sometimes feel you in my body. When I feel you, my heart beats faster /
my muscles tense up / I find it hard to breathe / ....
(fill in how you respond physically to your difficult feeling)

Now I know what you feel like, I am going to accept your presence. I'm even
going to welcome you in!

I can practise saying 'At the moment I feel this difficult emotion' to remind myself that it is temporary, rather than saying 'I am the difficult feeling'.

I realise that you don't always stick around for long. You are like a cloud drifting by. Usually I no longer feel this feeling after ....

....

If you don't disappear, I will accept your presence and be gentle with myself.

I have found these strategies help me when this feeling comes up.

Love,

....

(25.)

FINDING THE POSITIVES

Negative emotions are not necessarily bad. While scientists have many theories about how many emotional systems we have, I find the three-system model developed by Professor Paul Gilbert the easiest to follow. We have a threat system that includes emotions of anger, fear and disgust, which help us to identify dangers in the world; then a drive system, linked to excitement and joy, which motivates us; and finally a soothing system, which is linked to feelings of calm and safety, and which allows us to care for, and receive care from, others. The key point is that all three systems evolved to allow us to survive, and all three are important.

Armed with this knowledge, I find it easier to rethink what I previously considered dark emotions. They are a natural and necessary part of the way humans are wired, and without emotions we would have no sense of values or what matters to us. Even supposedly rational decisions made by our cognitive brain are often based on our emotions. The Cartesian division between rational (our thinking brain) and irrational (our emotional brain) suggested by the French philosopher and scientist René Descartes (thus its name) is oversimplified. Both influence each other.

Emotions can also be a positive force for change – we can indeed sing in the rain! Sadness, for instance, can be a sign we may need to withdraw and signal to our loved ones that we need help. Fear can lead to us finding our courage. Guilt can motivate us to reach out to others. While being angry is natural, it can be expressed safely and can even be harnessed in a good way as energy for causes we care about. Often social change is fuelled by anger at the status quo. For instance, anger about the stigma around mental illness has led to more acceptance.

If, for example, you were feeling angry at work right now, you could acknowledge your moment of anger and say to yourself, 'I am having a moment of feeling furious with my boss,' and then move to, 'I will harness my anger to make sure some important things change in the office'. If you were feeling sad, instead of saying 'I am miserable,' you could accept a moment of sadness and then say, 'I will allow myself some quiet time to chat to someone about how I am feeling, and I will become closer to that person in the process, which wouldn't have happened if I hadn't been feeling sad.' The magnet exercise on the next page is a good way to do this.

We appreciate the good times that follow even more by having experienced the bad. In fact, we would not appreciate sunnier times without living through the rainy ones. I love the way this idea is expressed in this poem by the 19th-century Scottish writer Charles Mackay.

See also *Belly breathing* on page 14.

Oh you tears,
I'm thankful that you run,
Though you trickle in the darkness,
You shall glitter in the sun
The rainbow could not shine if the rain refused to fall,
And the eyes that cannot weep are the saddest eyes of all.

Your turn to find something positive in a negative feeling by using a magnet:

● Place your fingertip on the negative side of the magnet.

● Focus on whatever emotion is troubling you as you place your finger on the negative charge. Say out loud what that feeling is.

● As you breathe in, imagine the breath going to the place where you feel discomfort or trouble. Imagine the in-breath bringing light to that area.

● Then as you breathe out, breathe out the negative feeling at the same time.

● While still having your finger on the negative charge of the magnet, spend a moment finding some positive aspect of that feeling. Say out loud what is positive about the feeling. You are not trying to deny the feeling but to find a positive interpretation of it.

● Then slowly trace along the shape of the magnet. As you do so, imagine the negative thought losing some of its negative charge as you allow for its more positive aspects.

● To help this process, keep breathing as you trace your finger. Breathe in your new positive thought, and breathe out any remaining negative thoughts.

● when you reach the positive end of the magnet, end the exercise by focusing just on your more positive interpretation of your negative thought.

● Repeat this exercise five times.

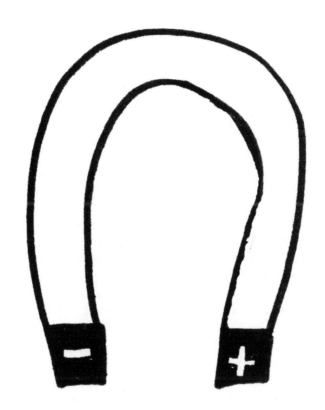

(26.)

CELEBRATING

As someone with school-age children, I am still in a world of milestones and congratulatory moments: certificates, the odd cup (well, one awarded to a son for his 'wit and wisdom') and graduation ceremonies. For me, less so. As we age, we are lucky if our achievements are marked by anything more than a quick drink in the pub. This is especially true if like me you are self-employed. Yet while I believe in enjoying the journey (see my thoughts on the *Being happy not perfect* on page 82), it is also important to celebrate our accomplishments, especially modest, everyday ones. There is much joy to be had in seeing and appreciating the ordinary.

It's hard to do so. Patting oneself on the back seems self-congratulatory and even arrogant. It can be even harder for sensitive and empathetic people to be their own cheerleaders. Unwilling to shine the spotlight on themselves, they tend to wait till someone else congratulates them. I will never forget the thrill I felt years ago when the editor of the newspaper I was working on sent me what we used to call a 'herogram' in the office. I can remember the exact words of his note

celebrating a news story I had written: 'Congratulations on your scoop on a subject of HUGE interest to our readers.' Scoop! I have the letter to this day.

In my new freelance life, I am unlikely to be getting any more herograms anytime soon. Instead, I have had to recognise my own achievements as part of developing more self-compassion and a kindlier, friendlier inner voice. Every time I want a bit of praise or encouragement from someone else, I see if I can find it in myself instead. This makes me feel powerful. I no longer have to wait for a kind word. I can say it myself!

Odd though it may sound, you can even send yourself a celebratory postcard to enjoy the moment twice: first when you write it, and second when you receive the card in the post. I know it might seem eccentric. This time I don't have the excuse that it is a custom in Denmark (which as we know is among the world's happiest countries), but a mini-celebration of this kind fixes a moment of glory in our minds, whether it's being patient with the office photo- copier, or completing a chapter of a book. Or being courageous in the face of everyday adversity.

Another way of not letting successes slip by is to record five things at the end of each day of which you are proud, be they waking early or having a lunchtime walk.

A last thought. Team up with others to make mini-celebrations more routine. When you go to an event or meet up for supper, share something positive that has happened. You might want to recognise others publicly at meetings to get everyone in the habit of celebrations, or have a 'celebration buddy' with whom you can share small triumphs more quietly. My dog, Sammy, performs the role beautifully, I find.

Your turn to get in the habit of recognising your own achievements:

1. Reflect for a moment on a recent achievement, however small. Take a moment to savour that feeling rather than brush it off, and congratulate yourself.

2. Decide on five things you can congratulate yourself for at the end of each day.

1.

2.

3.

4.

5.

3. Write yourself a postcard – fill in the one below, stick it in an envelope and don't forget to post it to yourself.

4. At the next social meal, whether at home or work, raise your glass and propose a toast. Prompt everyone around the table to do the same and to volunteer one thing they have achieved recently. Everyone will congratulate each other, I suspect!

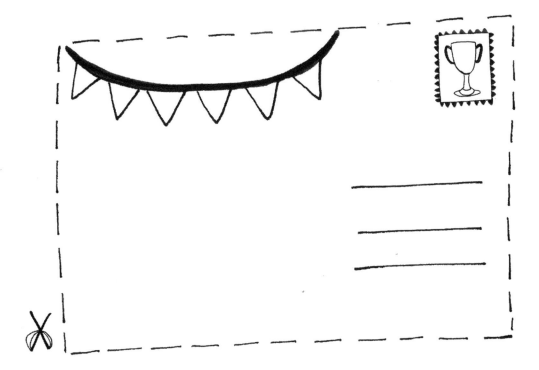

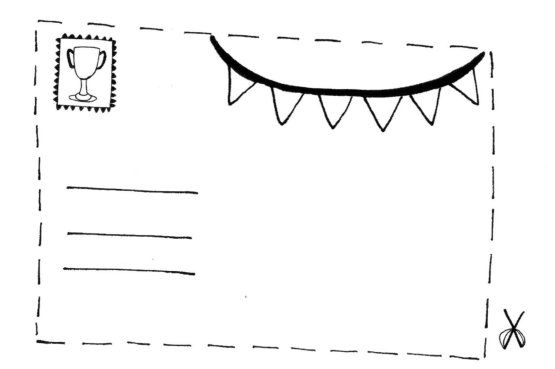

5. Pair up with someone else, maybe a friend, family member or colleague. Tell them three things you are proud of and ask them to do the same. You could record these wins, big or small, in the rosettes below.

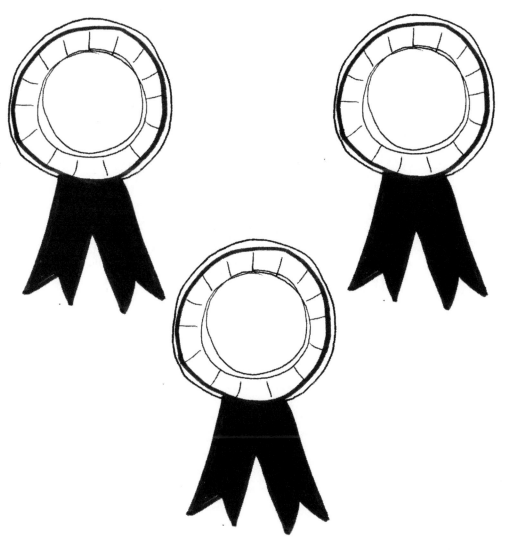

SECOND
APPRECIATION
PAUSE

Recognising people we normally overlook

Another moment to stop and reflect on all the work you have done so far. Congratulations. It can be easy to fail to enjoy the journey, as so often our eyes are on the prize. This appreciation pause is similar in some ways. It's about appreciating those you wouldn't routinely thank or notice in the busy rush to get things done. It could be the person at the till who serves you lunch, the office cleaner, the teacher who helped you solve a problem after class, a doctor who worked out why you haven't been feeling well or the police officer patrolling your neighbourhood. Take a moment to think of all these people in your life, people who admittedly are just doing their jobs, but as a result you may have overlooked them or taken them for granted. As you pause before the next set of activities, consider how our lives would fall apart without these individuals who look after our health, education, community and environment. Perhaps in the future you will make a point of thanking them. While this appreciation pause is designed to consider those you don't know well, it also works well for long-term partners and close friends and family members whom we often also overlook! Pause for a final moment to think about them too and quietly say thank you in your head.

EXPANDING YOUR RANGE

(27.)

TAKING A PAUSE

This morning, I was typing up notes for an article I was researching. Well, I was trying to. My laptop was rebelling. It kept stalling and my documents kept crashing. Finally, the computer decided it was time to switch itself off while it updated its software. There was nothing I could do but wait.

I decided to fill the time by biking to the Post Office. Once again, I was forced to pause, this time because I couldn't work my new fancy lock to secure my cycle outside. The quicker I tried to work the lock, the stiffer it became. I was forced to wheel it inside the Post Office and keep an eye on it while I waited in line. Which I then did, till I was almost at the head of the queue. Then an official asked me to move my bike, so I lost my slot.

At times when we are forced to wait, our goal-driven lives mean we can feel frustrated. We are not cracking through our to-do lists in a way that makes us feel constructive and purposeful. This is even more the case if we wait without our phones: there isn't really any downtime now, just phone time.

Yet these moments when we are forced to pause can have their own magic to them, if we receive them in a different way. We can decide that the frustrations we are experiencing are areas in our lives on which we need to work. Stuck in line at the Post Office? Perhaps right now you need to deepen your capacity for patience, precisely because you are a resistant student. (It's true, I do and I am!) To reverse the usual cliché, don't just do something, stand there.

If this feels challenging, there are a few other habits I have adopted to make waiting easier and more enjoyable. One is to consider that waiting can be a chance to look around and notice, 'to stand and stare' as W.H. Davies puts it in his poem 'Leisure,' which has helped me rethink downtime.

Another strategy is to pause deliberately, rather than because you are forced to by an irritating bike padlock or a crashing computer. Think of it as putting down a deposit in the patience bank – you can then cope better when life forces you to make an inevitable withdrawal.

Another way of embracing that moment of downtime is to enjoy the stillness positively.

At first you will notice how hard it is to

do nothing when you are impatient. You are furious at being stopped in your tracks. Then slowly become more aware of each of your senses in turn – use the path exercise on the opposite page to help you do this. Notice your breathing and thoughts and how your impatience begins to subside. If you need to challenge your thoughts, remind yourself that you will be in a better frame of mind when you are no longer consumed with impatient rage. If you can't focus, try writing with your non-dominant hand as another exercise in slowing down.

Combine these strategies, and you may not only accept forced moments of downtime, but actively enjoy them too. They are good short-term fixes. And in time, when combined with meditation or conscious breathing, they may lead to a deeper shift to becoming a more patient person. As W.H. Davies puts it so well:

A poor life this if, full of care,
We have no time to stand and stare.

Your turn to slow down and enjoy the downtime:

1. Slowly trace your finger along this wavy path and follow the prompts as you do so:

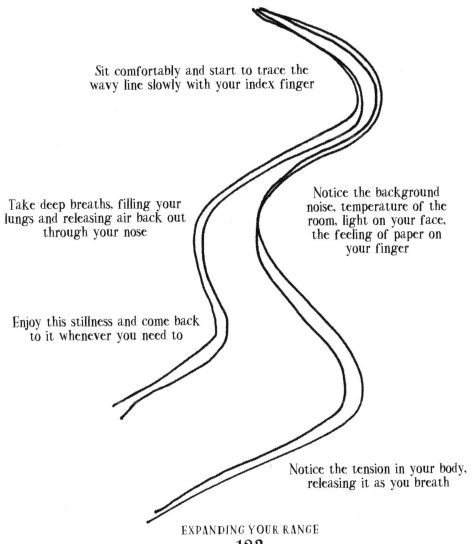

Sit comfortably and start to trace the wavy line slowly with your index finger

Notice the background noise, temperature of the room, light on your face, the feeling of paper on your finger

Take deep breaths, filling your lungs and releasing air back out through your nose

Enjoy this stillness and come back to it whenever you need to

Notice the tension in your body, releasing it as you breath

2. With your non-dominant hand, try writing your name in the box on this page. Notice how it feels to go at half your normal speed.

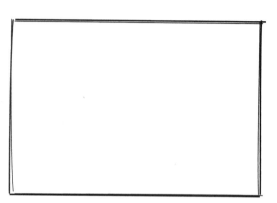

3. Learn this poem 'Leisure' by W.H. Davies to recite whenever you are stuck in a queue:

What is this life if, full of care,
We have no time to stand and stare.
No time to stand beneath the boughs
And stare as long as sheep and cows.
No time to see, when woods we pass,
Where squirrels hide their nuts in grass.
No time to see, in broad daylight,
Streams full of stars, like skies at night.
No time to turn at Beauty's glance,
And watch her feet, how they can dance.
No time to wait till her mouth can
Enrich that smile her eyes began?
A poor life this if, full of care,
We have no time to stand and stare.

(28.)

BALANCING ROLES

We all embrace multiple selves, be it our work self, our family self or our sporting self (less developed in my own case). I know I enjoy life when I find time in my life for all of my different roles. Over-develop one side of our personality, and we can become unbalanced. It's rather like a bird with an unduly strong right wing, which leaves it in danger of flying round and round in circles.

So while it's generally healthy to feel integrated and whole, I have found it handy to imagine that I can also play different roles, each of which needs some time in the diary. This kind of compart-mentalising is a skill mastered by many in order to maintain balance. Forensic anthropologists (who dissect dead bodies) are taught to use this skill to complete their work with no emotional connection. They reject any guilt or sadness they may feel relating to the death of the body they are investigating. Social workers, doctors and police officers do the same.

I too try and limit my responsibilities to their different compartments. One way of doing so is to give myself different names and symbols for the different aspects of my personality. For my parent role, I think of myself as Mum. This is the me who does the school run, goes to parent meetings, sorts multi-coloured unmatching socks, and remembers we need more washing-up liquid. She is also a person who hugs and hopes for cards on Mother's Day. The symbol for this might be me sitting at the end of a child's bed chatting to them.

At work, I am Rachel Kelly. This is the person who is grown up, or tries to be. She wants to be told she's doing a good job even though she sends herself postcards saying just that. This Rachel wants to be professional and trustworthy. The symbol would be me dressed in one of the crisp white shirts I favour when working.

With friends and when I'm socialising, I am Rach. This is someone who is happiest in box-fresh trainers and high-waisted soft cotton dark blue jeans, someone who loves having people round to supper and sending them poems if they have fallen in love or lost a parent. She tries to support others, but likes having fun too. This Rach is to be found at a corner table in a café, sharing something delicious and having a laugh with a pal.

And then there's just Rachel, who likes being on her own with her dog. She enjoys pottering in the garden, deadheading the browning geraniums and wondering what to do about the lily beetles ravaging her plants. She enjoys contemplating the passing seasons. The symbol for this me would be a picture of me walking Sammy.

Being conscious of these roles has helped me fully inhabit my different identities, and potentially switch roles if that's appropriate. Sometimes, when I am distressed, I try and figure out which aspect of me is dominant, and is that appropriate? There's nothing worse than being in my professional work mode when a child needs some attention.

When I plan my diary, a good day is now one where all my different roles get a look-in. This might combine some work (Ms Kelly) with an afternoon alone (Rachel), and then some drinks in the evening (Rach) before time at home (Mum). I don't actually write in my different names alongside different events in the diary, but thinking in this way has made my diary-planning sessions easier and led to more variety and balance. Sammy is pleased too, as it means he does not get forgotten.

Your turn to think about your different roles and how they all need time and space for a balanced life:

In each of the juggling balls below, draw an image that symbolises one of your identities. It could be a picture of you, or something you associate with that role in your life. So your work compartment might have a backpack or briefcase; your fun and friends personality might include a cocktail glass. Then write underneath the name you use for each of your different roles. You may want to draw an extra ball for an extra role. Use this classification of your different selves when you are planning your diary in future. Every time you schedule an event, remind yourself which role you will inhabit and which compartment you are in.

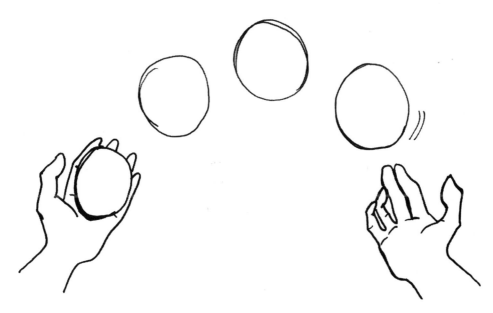

(29.)

SEEING AFRESH

It's the weekend, and a cousin has brought her three-year-old daughter, Hannah, for lunch. She is playing with our pink pig salt shaker on the kitchen table, piling up mounds of white crystals. Despite the mess she is making, there's something wonderful about her delight in this simple thing. Inspired by Hannah, I try and look at a salt shaker as if seeing it for the first time. I marvel at the efficiency of its design, the ease with which the salt flows through, and the way the crystals catch the light. Before it was just something small and pink.

I'm stealing this idea of noticing everyday stuff in a new light from the Buddhist concept of 'beginner's mind', from the word *shoshin*. The idea is to drop our expert's mind and preconceived notions and look at the world with curiosity and delight, as if it were brand new. The idea is usually linked to activities, but it is also a useful way to approach relationships. When we no longer have assumptions about what we expect from someone and behave as if we were meeting them for the first time, life can be much smoother. Ask my husband...

I now make a point of noticing and appreciating everyday objects. One of the easiest ways to do this is to deny yourself something you routinely use. See how much you appreciate a comfy chair after a few hours of continuous standing. Enjoy the way you sink into its cushions, the feel of the linen fabric on your bare legs. Observe the chair from a new perspective, as if you had come from another planet. Think about the ways it helps you. Imagine all those whose efforts went into making it, from the woodcutter, to the carpenter, to the designer, to the person who sold it to you from a shop.

This approach works equally well to renew a sense of delight in the miracle of our own bodies, which we often take for granted and neglect. Stop using your hands for a moment. Then appreciate the miracle of engineering that they are: some scientists believe that hands are the single most important development since our ancestors evolved from being chimpanzees to walking on two feet. Nearly all that our species has achieved has been with our hands, and not using them for a moment gives Hannah and me a chance to reflect on their remarkable adaptability. We had fun exploring things we could do with our hands, from clapping to counting on our fingers. Hannah's hands were delightfully rosy and plump, mine less so. But both of us, and me especially, ended our session with a real sense of exuberant appreciation. An added bonus is there may be some salt left over for lunch.

Your turn to notice everyday objects with a beginner's mind:

---

1. Think of an everyday object, and imagine you have just used this object for the first time ever. Perhaps you have come down from Mars.

What do you appreciate about it? In what ways does it help you?

....

....

....

....

Imagine how your day would go if this object didn't exist. How would it be inconvenient?

....

....

....

....

2. Use the space opposite to draw round your hand slowly. Think of all the ways you use your hands and be thankful for them. You could write on each finger something you appreciate about your hands, whether it's playing the piano or stroking your pet.

30.

TREE CLIMBING

This exercise isn't for everyone, as it is about climbing trees. Well, actually hauling up a tree is a more appropriate phrase, as that's what I did to clamber onto the lowest branch of a senior beech tree this week. Odd as it sounds, studies suggest our ancestors spent much of their lives up trees as we evolved from arboreal animals, so climbing may well feel quite instinctive. But of course some of you might find the prospect daunting or be physically unable to do so. If this is the case, you will still be able to complete the exercise, which is also about the perspective trees can give us.

So here I am, astride a smooth grey branch in the middle of a field. Not quite as comfortable as my favourite armchair, admittedly, but my berth brings other blessings. I feel protected by the canopy of lime green leaves above me. They smell sweet and earthy, a scent which comes from the essential oils the plants are emitting for their own antifungal and antibacterial protection. My lungs are enjoying breathing the less polluted air, filtered by those same leaves. In addition, my arms and legs get a good stretch when

I venture to climb a bit further: branches are excellent monkey bars.

Another blessing is that it is impossible to be on my phone. It's important to separate work from home life in a world where the two are co-mingled. Therefore, in my spare time I have taken up activities that can't be combined with office life or spending time on my phone, like swimming. Tree climbing is even better as it gets me outside.

Cutting ourselves off from nature harms us. The term *Shinrin-yoku*, meaning 'forest bathing', was introduced in Japan by the Forest Agency of the Japanese government in 1982. Studies show that a walk in the woods reduces pain and diminishes stress. My version is forest climbing: being actually up a tree, embraced by its branches, enhances and intensifies all these benefits for me. I am fully immersed in the experience.

Things look different from a higher vantage point, albeit that I am only a couple of metres or so above the ground. I have no choice but to concentrate when I am climbing a tree, for safety reasons, which cuts out extraneous, mind-cluttering concerns. Robert Macfarlane, the nature writer, says that the Welsh phrase, *dod yn ôl at fy nghoed*, means to return to a balanced state of mind. It also literally means, 'to return to my trees'. So, psychologically, I feel calmer. Also, trees challenge our imagination. There is nothing monotonous or repetitive about climbing; every tree requires a different game plan.

But of all the many physical and psychological advantages of tree climbing that I have outlined, the greatest of them all is this: a tree is a metaphor for life. So, sitting in my tree, I think of its roots. Then I ponder what roots me in my own life; what keeps my tree steady when the storm comes and stops it from upending? I think about the steadiness my family gives me; I think about my work and how it provides structure to my day. I think of those who have been there for me when my mother started her chemotherapy earlier this year.

Next I think about the branches of the tree. Who could I reach out to, like the branches on a tree? Are there people in my life I could be in touch with? Might I branch out myself, and become more adventurous?

Then I think about the leaves, which provide shade and, when they fall, enrich the ground beneath. What am I giving back to the world? Then I think about the trunk of the tree, and how I need to keep strengthening my own back, which is weak from too much sitting at a desk and not always following my own advice about watching my posture (see *Sitting and standing* on page 43). I need to stand tall in order to reach, give back and thrive.

I think about a tree's ability to bend under pressure. When there are strong winds, a tree never stays in its upright position. If it did, it could break. If we stay upright during challenging times, we could also snap. Instead, we must bend, feel sad, cultivate an understanding and kindly voice to ourselves, so that when the storm calms, we can lift ourselves upright again.

On which note I realise it is getting dark and it is time to saunter home. I climb down, choosing an oval leaf to take with me. I admire its torpedo shape, silky hairs and wavy edge. It will be a nice reminder of a happy day spent up high.

Your turn to reach new heights and alter your perspective:

1. For those who can climb: oak and hornbeam are strong, while willow and poplar are less robust. Enjoy the feeling of a strong trunk supporting you. Climb as high as you dare, but the first branch is fine.

2. If you can't climb a tree, find one to admire. Look up to its tallest point and watch its leaves and branches sway in the wind. Wrap your arms around the trunk and enjoy the feeling as your face is pressed against the bark. Feel and enjoy the branches' scents, colours and smells.

3. Try imagining a tree as a metaphor for your own life. Thinking about a tree can help us visualise our own lives and give us perspective on what matters to us, and how we can understand ourselves. Take each part of the tree in turn and connect it to your own life. Write down your reflections under the questions opposite.

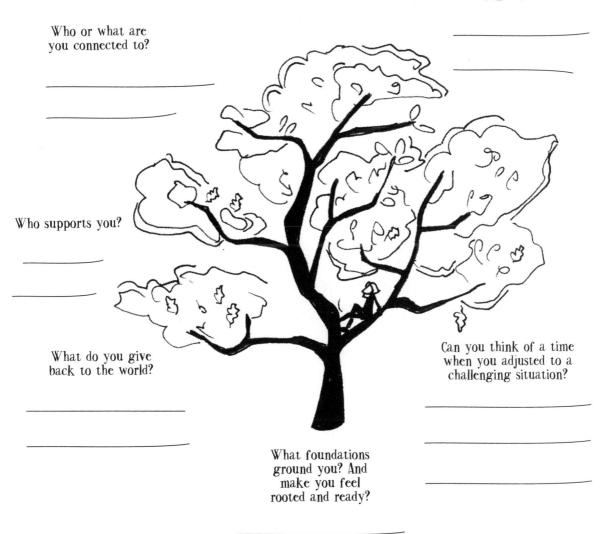

How would you
branch out?

_____

_____

_____

Who or what are
you connected to?

_____

_____

Who supports you?

_____

_____

What do you give
back to the world?

_____

_____

Can you think of a time
when you adjusted to a
challenging situation?

_____

_____

_____

What foundations
ground you? And
make you feel
rooted and ready?

_____

_____

4. Use this book as a leaf press. Choose two or three beautiful leaves that you come across whilst you are climbing or admiring the tree, or anytime you find yourself outside. Close and weigh the book down with heavy books or other items and leave for about a week. When you return to the page, you will have papery pressed leaf.

PLACE YOUR LEAVES ON THE NEXT PAGE AND CLOSE THE BOOK GENTLY. KEEP CLOSED FOR SEVEN DAYS.

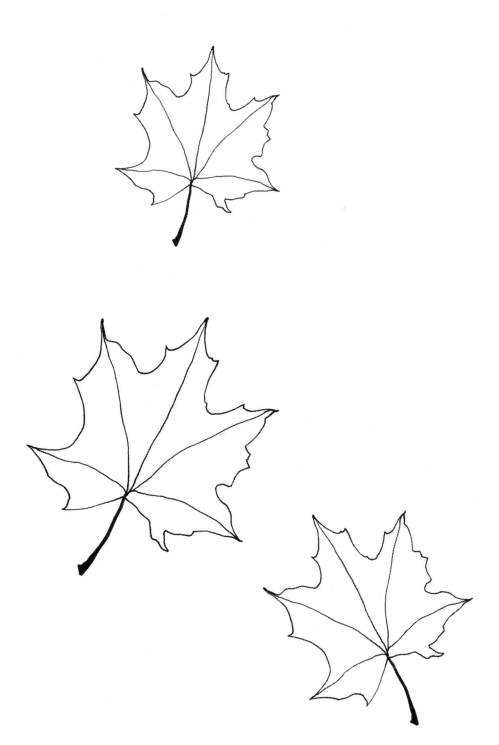

31.

SKETCHING NATURE

When did you last touch a velvety petal? Or linger over the sight of dandelion seeds whirling in the air? Or appreciate the sound of pigeons cooing? Not recently enough, is the answer for many of us. Walls too often surround us as we breathe air-conditioned air and sit under artificial lights, marooned in a sea of roads. Somehow we must discover pockets of the natural world even in the midst of the concrete landscape most of us inhabit. We have an innate tendency to connect with nature, honed over millions of years and known as biophilia. But, given the reality of our urban lives today, we may need to focus actively on being attentive to nature's healing powers. Many of us suffer from 'nature deficit disorder', a phrase coined by the writer Richard Louv in 2005. It has no medical basis but it did strike a chord with me.

One answer for me is drawing nature in the city. As modest as my efforts are, I find sketching the natural world amplifies its known relaxing effects. I know others prefer to photograph signs of nature, and research suggests they enjoy higher levels of joy than those who photograph man-made objects, but I find drawing is a lovely grounding and expressive exercise. We are forced to notice our subject in order to capture its essence on the paper.

I like returning to the same spots to draw so I can appreciate the changing seasons, in themselves a comfort as the shrivelled brown leaves recover greenness each year. And I like small drawings: that's why you will find that the space for your sketch on the next page is tiny, as a big, empty page can be off-putting and daunting. Small I can manage.

Nature looks different when I draw. I discover a new appreciation for the extraordinary to be found in the most ordinary twig or flower or bird. Have you noticed that what initially seems like a grey pigeon has all sorts of iridescent purple and blue feathers around its neck, which sparkle in the light? (That's what I observed today.) Even though I am concentrating on a small patch of nature for my drawing, I observe my wider surroundings with more attention, too. On my walk home, I notice the delicate veining of a leaf, or see the contours of the bark on a neighbouring tree as if for the first time (see *Playing like a child* on page 57). I see patterns in the colours of the rain glistening on a spider's web. The more I look, the more I see.

An added bonus is it's almost impossible not to see progress in your creative efforts. Few other activities offer such a prompt return in terms of personal satisfaction, or do so more inexpensively, than drawing. It's sociable too: the art on the page is like a hand held out to connect with others who stop to chat and ask about the picture.

I know that for some people, drawing makes them feel stressed. If this is the case for you, think of it as doodling to take the pressure off. Or you might wish to jot down any details you notice about a bird or a leaf, rather than attempt to draw it. Easier still, care for a plant instead. Good indoor choices include a peace lily plant, which removes common household airborne chemicals; or *sansevieria*, also known as the snake plant. Like all plants, these are beneficial in the way they absorb carbon dioxide and chemicals, and pump out oxygen. What's not to like?

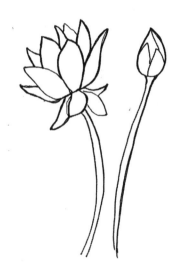

Your turn to harness nature for relaxation:

1. Wrap up warmly if need be.

2. Gather a pen or pencil and this book; you may need something to sit on, preferably waterproof.

3. Go to your nearest green space or just find a tree, or bush, or some plants if you are stuck in an urban jungle.

4. Find a spot and make yourself comfortable.

5. Choose an object to sketch: there are a couple of suggestions in the box opposite. Focus on that object for a few minutes, observing it as closely as you can. Enjoy noticing every natural detail.

6. Close your eyes. Try and remember every detail of your chosen object.

7. Open your eyes and look at it again. Keep looking, and fill in the sketch in the box opposite. Just let your hand follow what your eye sees. Try not to let your eyes wander elsewhere, or lift your pencil from the paper.

8. Next time you go sketching, find another object to sketch.

9. If sketching isn't your thing, you could jot down in each box a detail you have noticed about your chosen subject.

10. On your way back home or to your office, buy a plant for your desk so you can bring nature inside.

A BIRD	AN INSECT

(32.)

FINDING FLOW

The last hour has whizzed by. I have been writing an article, fiddling with the sentences to get my thoughts in order, doing a task that engaged me. The creative immersion was complete. When I emerged, blinking, I was amazed that 60 minutes had passed as it felt more like ten. I reflected on how happy it felt to have been in the flow.

This may sound rather unexciting, but the idea of flow is anything but dull. A Hungarian-American psychologist called Mihaly Csikszentmihalyi invented the concept: (a bonus for anyone who can pronounce his name properly – answer on the opposite page*). He found that people are happiest when doing demanding but ultimately manageable tasks. The tasks are neither so difficult they are stressful, nor so easy they are boring. They become an end in themselves. (See also *Playing like a child* on page 57). Our minds settle in a happy, focused way on this middle ground. By contrast, when our mind is distracted, Csikszentmihalyi suggests that we are less happy than when we are present. Unfortunately, he says our mind is distracted around 50 per cent of the time if we don't make an effort to concentrate in this way.

There are two aspects to finding your own sense of flow: first, choosing the right task to do, and second, doing it in the right way. Whatever activity you choose, the challenge is not to quit at the start. Because your journey into being in the flow often starts with a struggle. While I loved writing my article, when I began it I was stressed. I wondered if it would make any sense. Only after 15 minutes or so did I relax, and then believe I could manage the task.

The second element is how you engage with the task you have chosen. This is hard in a world in which we are almost permanently doing six things at once. Do a little test on yourself to see how many times you check your phone over just ten minutes. Some studies suggest it takes us 15 minutes to get back in the flow once we have been interrupted. So carve out a time when you can fully focus. I need at least an hour in which to do so, though it is difficult to judge exact timings. One of the features of being in the flow is that time is distorted.

To maximise your chance of being focused, start with some alternate nostril breathing: you can try out this technique by following the steps in the next exercise. This helps create a calm flow state by balancing your autonomic nervous system, the part of your nervous system responsible for automatic functions such as breathing, the heartbeat and digestion. Breathing through your right nostril is connected to your sympathetic response, the confusingly named stress response. Breathing through your left nostril is connected to your parasympathetic response. Many of us have an overly active sympathetic system, so this breathing exercise helps us to rebalance and is a good preparation for being in the flow.

You are lucky if what you do for a living starts to feel like a pleasure in this way. If it doesn't, see if there are other times when you can be in the flow, like when cooking or exercising. Use the excercises overleaf to spark some ideas.

*This is how you pronounce Mihaly Csikszentmihalyi's name: Me-high Cheeks-sent-me-high.

Now your turn to be in the moment and fully experience the task at hand:

1. Note down some activities you enjoy when you are absorbed and time flies. These are activities that come easily even if at first there's an element of challenge.

....

....

....

....

2. Set aside time this week for one of your chosen activities, even making a note in your diary.

3. Before you start, do the alternate nostril breathing exercise to get yourself in the right mood.

a) Find a comfortable seat.

b) Close your right nostril with your right thumb. (You will just be using your right hand throughout.)

c) Inhale deeply through your left nostril.

d) At the top of your inhalation, close your left nostril with the ring finger of the same right hand as you release the right nostril.

e) Exhale through your right nostril.

f) Keeping the left nostril closed, inhale deeply through your right nostril.

g) Seal your right nostril again with your thumb, and then release your left nostril.

h) Exhale out of your left nostril. You should now be in the original position, with your thumb sealing your right nostril. This is one cycle.

i) Balance your inhalations and exhalations so they are the same length through both nostrils.

j) Repeat up to ten full cycles, gradually increasing the number of repetitions as you gain experience.

4. Get started! Spend at least an hour on your activity.

● How relaxed do you feel afterwards on a scale of one to ten?

1 2 3 4 5 6 7 8 9 10

● Did you lose your sense of time?

YES / NO

33.

BEING A FRIEND

My goddaughter and I have been chatting as we sip cups of pale gold camomile tea. She recounted her day spent doing work experience at our local hospital. On the ward rounds, a doctor remarked on how the atmosphere can vary depending on the temperament of the patients. Even just one cheery patient can lift the spirits of the entire ward, as was the case today thanks to an elderly patient called Laurence who resembled Father Christmas with his curly white hair and beard. His jolly spirit, kindness and compassion to others meant the other patients on his ward were noticeably smilier.

Our emotions are contagious: it's known that happy couples become more temperamentally alike as the years go by, because humans reflect each other's expressions. Our personalities converge and we pick up each other's feelings, in the same way that Laurence's upbeat spirit cheered up the ward. Studies confirm that peope who are surrounded by happy people show increases in their own happiness over time. The reverse is also true: being around those who are negative can make you feel worse.

Laurence is what my goddaughter and I decided we would name a 'light giver'. He's the type of person who:

1. Makes you laugh.
2. Is present for you at both negative and positive times of your life.
3. When you suggest something, has a contribution to make.
4. Interacts with you in a way that brings out your most authentic self.
5. Accepts you for who you are in the moment without suggesting you change.

How then to make sure we have more supportive light-giving people in our lives? Counter-intuitively, the answer is to become more like Laurence. While we can't control others, we can do something about our own behaviour. Having better friends is about becoming a better friend. Do we make others laugh? Are we there for our friends when something goes wrong for them and able to engage in meaningful conversations with them? Are our friends able to be themselves or are we trying to change them, or complaining about them behind their backs? In short, what kind of friend are we?

Not always a good one in my case. But when I am more of a light giver, I find that others often reciprocate. Perhaps it's because people see positivity in us, like a mirror, and reflect it back. Or perhaps it's because of the energy that is then created between two people.

I say often, as this is not always easy. Reciprocity implies an equal two-way street between friendly individuals. Actually, it would be truer to say friendships are more usually unbalanced. There have been times when I have been heavily leant on. At other times I have relied greatly on friends myself, especially when I was unwell and unable to reciprocate. None of us can always be Laurences.

At times like this, sometimes all I have been able to do is to say thank you to those who have lightened my own periods of darkness, either with a card, or more surprisingly by making a simple badge with the word 'thank you' and their name on the front. This may sound like a childish thing to do, but this gesture seems to bring pleasure since it is so unexpected. My goddaughter resolved to make a card for Laurence.

Your turn to become more of a 'light giver' and appreciate those who bring light into your own life:

1. In the box below, look at your relationship with friends with whom you currently spend the most time. For each friend in turn, look at your relationship. Do you support them in the five light-giving ways? Fill in the form below. You could use percentages. You may prefer to make your own list of qualities that you find 'light givers' possess. If this is the case, think of the times when someone else's company has elevated your mood. What qualities in the person affected you? Adjust the table below to reflect your own list.

Friend's name	Do we laugh together?	Am I present for them when good and bad things happen?	When they suggest something do I contribute to their ideas?	Do I feel my authentic self with them?	Am I willing to accept them for who they are in any given moment?	How could I make the friendship more light-giving if needed?

If you find your answers are near 100 per cent, congratulations. But if the answers are dropping below 70 per cent, you may want to think more about how you could become a better friend, or if those people are the best friends for you.

2. Now jot down more names of people you feel you could be more of a genuinely good friend to:

-
-
-
-

3. Come back to this list in a few months, and see if you have managed to support these friends in the five light-giving ways.

4. Make a badge for a friend to say thank you for their support for those times when you are unable to do much more.

● Cut out the shapes opposite.

● Make a hole where the black circle is with a hole-puncher.

● Write thank you and their name on the front of the badge and then decorate it.

● Attach a safety pin to the back with Sellotape.

● Give it to a friend who is a light giver in your life.

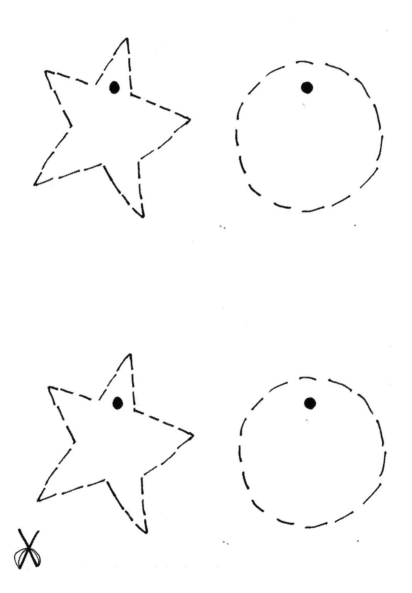

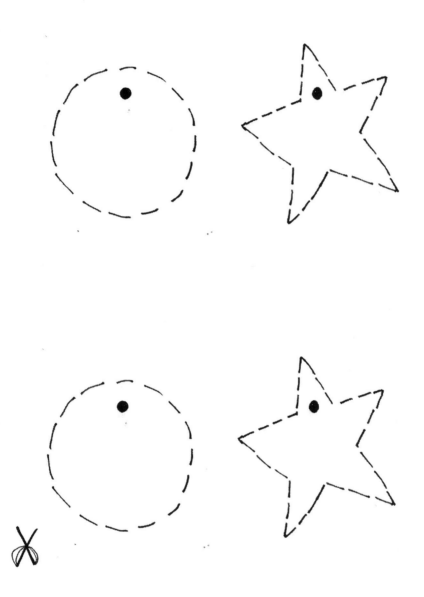

32.

WRITING POETRY

You might never have considered writing a poem, and indeed the thought might make you want to turn this page. But studies have linked good psychological health with creativity. Research suggests that GPs who prescribed arts activities to some of their patients saw a drop in hospital admission.

In the same way that an artist spills their feelings onto the page, writing a poem can pin down good times, as well as make sense of adversity and anaesthetise trauma. My head may be full of chaotic pain, but I find the chaos lessens when I get my thoughts onto the page. At least I have created something concrete and tangible out of a swirling and shapeless darkness in my mind. It feels like building a well when previously all I could see was desert.

If the thought of writing a poem daunts you, make the process less agonising by giving yourself a time limit. Don't worry about rhyming or scansion or rhythm or if the poem is any good. (See also *Being happy not perfect* on page 82.)

Instead, write straight from the heart: poetry is as much about how you feel as the words you choose and the images they suggest. Sometimes that feeling is physical, held somewhere in my body. Sometimes the feeling is suggested by a simple phrase, like my mother saying 'I have had a good run' which I used in a poem about her being unwell. Sometimes the emotion occurs as a strong image. Recently for example, a boy in a yellow T-shirt flying a kite summed up happiness. So did the sight of a man in a purple tracksuit practising shooting a ball into a makeshift goal, despite the roughness of the grass and the lack of any posts in the park.

If you want some help on structure, you might create two characters in the poem. This is particularly helpful if I am trying to make sense of something troubling. One character can personify whatever is bothering you, the other a character you identify with. Write a poetic dialogue between the two, whereby the character you embody ends up feeling empowered.

I wrote my own poem after a visit to mum in hospital where she was having chemotherapy.

GROWING UP – *By Rachel Kelly, February 2018*

And will I ever feel grown-up?
And what does that mean?
Up to where?
Grown to what?
I feel as I have always felt
Unsure, uncertain, still a child
Yet now another,
To my own mother,
Who stumbles now
And grips my hand
As once I gripped hers.
'I have had a good run,'
My mother says
But my run with you
Has only just begun, I want to shout!
You can't leave me now!
The drugs must work!
But I say nothing.
How can I complain
When hers is a life of pain?
Of scraped retinas and
Catheters, and chemo?
'I have had a good run,' she says,
But who will hold my hand?
I want to shout
Even as I lend my arm
To take her back to bed.
For I am the grown-up now.

See also *Being happy not perfect* on page 82.

Now your turn to use poetry to make sense of events, both good and bad:

1. Set a timer for a maximum of 15 minutes.

2. Don't worry about rhyming or the rhythm of each line. Just write from the heart.

3. Take note of whatever is happening for you in this moment.

- Is your head full of thoughts?
- Or are bodily sensations grabbing your attention?
- Is something you are seeing or smelling taking centre stage?
- Do you feel the emotion somewhere in your body?
- How does it feel?
- Does it have a colour or shape?
- Does it smell or make a sound?

4. Is there an image that occurs to you that sums up how you are feeling?

5. Is there a line of dialogue which sums up how you are feeling?

6. You could use this first line as a prompt... Either.... 'The sky darkened' or 'The sky lightened...'

7. Could you create two people in your poem to discuss whatever dilemma it is you are writing about?

8. Write first, worry second. It's better to get something down than agonise over whether what you are doing is any good.

9. If you find it easier, you could use the structure of an acrostic poem to help give your poem form. I've given an example on the next page. You write down a word vertically, then use each letter as a prompt for that line of your poem.

10. If a poem doesn't come naturally, do not worry. You could try jotting down a simple line which expresses how you are feeling instead.

11. If you are still suffering from writer's block, set a timer for three minutes and write continuously – about anything and everything to help generate ideas.

Use this space to write your poem:

Or... write an acrostic poem using the first letters of these words to guide you.

A ....   F ....   F ....

N ....   E ....   U ....

X ....   A ....   N ....

I ....   R ....

E ....

T ....

Y ....

(35.)

TAKING BACK CONTROL

In the 1970s, the Australian scientist Michael Marmot decided to investigate workplace stress and believed he had found the perfect environment in which to do so: the British civil service, based in Whitehall. Who was more likely to have a stress-related heart attack? The boss at the top or somebody below him? Everyone assumed it would be the permanent secretary, in my mind marching purposely with a black furled umbrella and bowler hat, who would be burdened by having so much responsibility.

In fact Marmot's results revealed the lower the employee ranked in terms of hierarchy, the higher their stress levels and, in turn, likelihood of having a heart attack. The scientist discovered that the less control a person has over their work, the more likely they are to become stressed and, importantly, depressed.

So people with less control feel more stressed. What's the solution? Tricky, I agree, short of changing jobs, which may be something we all need to consider from time to time. But there are steps you can take to change your mind-set to feel more powerful, even in challenging environ-ments. I'm the first to admit this is hard. But you have to believe you have power over your life, because you do.

The first step is to identify when you find yourself slipping into victim mode. Typically, when I'm feeling rudderless, I find myself believing that my successes or failures are because of things I can't do anything about, like luck or the DNA I was born with, rather than hard work and practice. You need to challenge your belief that you can't make a difference. You can.

One way I can regain this sense of power is to make some quick small changes through my daily routine, the first being to make my bed to my own satisfac-tion, the white duvet perfectly aligned and my pillows nicely plumped. The act of achieving and controlling something as soon as you wake up puts you in the right mood to continue a sense of control throughout your day. The examples may not seem significant, but the act of taking control of small decisions in this way will give you confidence in your own power to affect larger decisions. Powerful business-men and women and politicians often adopt these tactics to establish a sense of control when entering a boardroom or unfamiliar environment. They might change the position of a glass, or alter the height of the microphone on a pulpit, or reshuffle the papers in front of them.

Another step is to watch your language, and think how you could rephrase statements about your own powerlessness. Language itself can make us feel more of a victim and gives our power to others. So instead of saying, 'I'm at the mercy of my mother-in-law', you might say, 'I can choose how to respond to my mother-in-law.' Perhaps the most useful word of all is 'yet.' So instead of saying, 'I can't deal with this', say 'I can't deal with this, yet.'

Making small changes and watching my language have made me feel more in control and therefore less stressed. If I forget the need to feel autonomous, I summon up the image of a Westminster mandarin complete with umbrella to remind myself of the Australian research. Thank you Mr Marmot.

See also *Managing time* on page 190.

Your turn to feel more in control:

1. On the left-hand page, write down how a usual day in your life plays out.

2. On the right-hand page, see if you can identify activities that could be adjusted. The idea is that you are in control of writing the story of your life, from what you do when you first get up to how you travel to work.

My daily routine

Changes I can make to feel more in control

P.T.O. for more ideas!

3. Try rephrasing some of these sentences: (rough answers are at bottom of the page)

1. I feel helpless in the office or home when my boss or partner criticises me.

....

....

2. I struggle to keep on top of the workload I am given.

....

....

3. I can't keep to deadlines.

....

....

4. My partner decides whether I am happy or not.

....

....

5. I can't say no.

....

....

Alternative more powerful phrases

1. I can choose how I respond in the office when my boss is mean to me.
2. I am learning how to keep on top of the workload I am given.
3. I can't keep to deadlines yet but I am practising and improving.
4. I am in control of my own destiny and can decide whether I allow someone else to determine my happiness.
5. It's a shame, I would love to help, but I am already committed.

(36.)

FEELING GOOD ENOUGH

Do you think you are fabulously likeable? Or do you feel more like a lowly worm? On a scale of zero to ten where zero is feeling that you are not good enough, and ten is feeling that you are fantastic, what would your score be?

When I first tried this exercise, which is recommended by the psychotherapist and hypnotherapist Rob Kelly, my score was unsurprisingly somewhere in the middle. Not quite a lowly worm, but not a glowworm either (as Churchill described himself in a letter to Violet Bonham Carter. 'We are all worms,' he wrote, 'But I do believe that I am a glowworm').

A few days later, however, my score plummeted from this mid-point. The reason was that an article I had written was rejected. Like many of us, how I feel about myself can alter, exhaustingly, depending on whether I am having a good or bad day. I'm quick to criticise myself and find fault with what I've done.

Over the years, I have established a kinder voice and more stable sense of self-worth, less dependent on the approval of others. (See also *Being kind to others* on page 70). I now am less at the

mercy of the inner voice that tells me I am not good enough, that I can't manage, and that I am powerless in the face of setbacks. This is the voice we might think of as our inner critic.

Our brains are naturally designed to be critical. As neuroscientist Dr Rick Hanson put it when describing what he called the 'negativity bias', our brains are like Velcro for negative experiences, and Teflon for positive ones. Evolution designed us in this way partly because focusing on what is wrong protected our tribe. (See also *Smiling and Laughing* on p.24). Our critical voice is there to protect us and make sure we don't make mistakes, so we aren't criticised and ostracised by others. So as a first step, do not blame yourself for having an inner critic. It has helped us evolve to this point.

The problem is that this critical faculty can often go into over-drive. I have learnt to moderate its voice. I have done this by first getting to know it, and noting its existing characteristics and the way it talks. Then I have made it a less scary presence by thanking it for the fact that it is trying to help, having a chat with it to explain that it could calm down a bit, and softening the way it appears in my head by giving it a humorous name (Cruella the Critic in my case!). This has created some distance between the two of us, as if the critic were a separate person rather than me.

Remind yourself that the limiting belief that we are not good enough is just a thought. How you feel about yourself isn't based on any objective reality so much as your own opinion, which crucially can change. We can all learn to be gentler and more self-compassionate. I do this by imagining what an inner friend would say if they replaced my inner critic. What would a kindly chum say over a cuppa?

There are two further steps I use to challenge in more detail my inner critic. The first is to discover whether it is telling the truth with a quick reality check (which is also useful when we mind-write, see page 210). Is it true that my article was poor? Could there be another explanation? More often than not I find what I think is the truth is actually my inner critic speaking rather than the objective reality. So it proved: the article was no longer relevant as the theme of that month's magazine had changed.

And second, can I find any positives in what has happened? In this case the time I had spent researching the article had been productive and I could use what I had learnt elsewhere. It is easy to ignore the good news when things go wrong: some of the other appreciation exercises in this book should help with this approach.

Adjusting your self-talk in this gentler, more measured way is important as scientists have found higher levels of self-compassion are associated with better health. When we respond to our personal failures, struggles and difficult circumstances with a kind and forgiving attitude, we enjoy a reduction in stress. We are also more likely to behave in a healthy way, eat sensibly, exercise, abstain from smoking, go to the doctor and follow doctor's orders. That's good enough for me.

See also *Celebrating* on page 112.

Your turn to deal with your current inner critic and replace it with a future inner critic who is more sympathetic:

1. Fill in the boxes below:

My current inner critic has these characteristics:	
Its name is:	
Its aim is:	
It makes me feel:	
It tends to appear when:	
It uses phrases such as:	

2. Now note down in more detail how you might change the way your inner critic appears to you:

My future inner critic could be more sympathetic:	
Its name could be: (Choose something humourous) Its aim could be: (Remind yourself that it's on your side)	
Its phrases could be softened in the following ways: (What would a friend say to you when your inner critic is in full flow?)	
Write down some new, kindlier phrases you might use when talking to your inner critic	

3. With this kindlier, gentle voice in your head, remember a recent encounter with your inner critic and ask yourself:

a) Was my inner critic telling the truth?

b) Were there any positives in what happened?

37.

DISCOVERING INSPIRATION

I first discovered the power of beautifully composed one-liners when I was ill with depression. I wasn't well enough to read a chapter, let alone a whole book. Instead, I derived comfort from soothing quotations, particularly a selection from our great poets and spiritual thinkers. One of my favourites was a line from the letter to the Corinthians by St Paul in the New Testament: 'My strength is made perfect in weakness.' It summed up much better than I could the idea that I would emerge stronger than before. Weakness and strength are part of one another. We cannot know one without the other, so they are both essential and are fortified for the presence of the other. This was a constructive thought when the whole episode felt so destructive. Actually, something good would come out of it.

Now I enjoy quotations from a wide variety of writers, actors, poets and thinkers, everything from 'You are a child of the universe, no more no less' from the poem 'Desiderata' (quoted in its entirety on my website) to 'I figure if a girl wants to be a legend, she should go ahead and be one' by the musical character Calamity Jane. I enjoy thinking about the words themselves and also feeling connected to whoever said them and borrowing their strength.

I enjoy interacting with quotations and inspiring messages in my everyday life by keeping them close, literally. The French philosopher Michel de Montaigne used to write his own inspiring quotations on the beams of his sitting room, where they still remain today. I do not have any beams to decorate, but I like writing out quotations in nice ink in a tidy script on a card decorated with an illustrated border. Elegant stationery can be as inspiring as the quote itself.

I also like propping up postcards round the house, be it on my bathroom mirror or the fridge, or collecting mugs and T-shirts and coasters with upbeat messages, I am never far from visible words which stir me. My latest favourites are bracelets, rings carved with inspiring lines and bookmarks.

As I have grown stronger, I have graduated from collecting up my one-liners, to sometimes learning inspiring verse by heart. Poetry has been my solace since I was a child. Whenever I feel uncertain or worried, I find reading about the experience of others reminds me I am not alone and gives me the words when I can't find them. Research suggests I am not alone. Studies agree that bibliotherapy can have a role to play in treating mental illness, though this is a relatively new area of research. I loved coming across the study that says people who read live an average of two years longer than those that don't pick up a book.

I like short poems or verses, and copying them out helps me remember them. Something in me is awakened during the process of committing the words to the page. Writing slows you down and gives you time to learn the lines. I learn what the poem is made of – each word and pause and line feels special. Its meaning is one that has become part of me.

Today I copied out a short verse from a longer poem by the Australian poet, politician and former police officer, Adam Lindsay Gordon. I like it because it was written in the 19th-century, so it reminds me how what is important doesn't change much over the centuries. It is also short; it rhymes; and I now know it by heart – as did the late Princess of Wales. Apparently it was her favourite poem.

Life is mostly froth and bubble,
Two things stand like stone.
Kindness in another's trouble,
Courage in your own.

Now your turn to decide on some favourite inspirational sayings to improve your state of mind:

1. Read through the sayings in the list below. Circle any that resonate with you.

'If more of us valued food and cheer and song above hoarded gold, it would be a merrier world.'
J.R.R. Tolkien, writer and poet (1892-1973)

'The mind is its own place, and in itself can make a Heaven of Hell, a Hell of Heaven.'
John Milton, poet (1608-1674)

To see a World in a Grain of Sand
And a Heaven in a Wild Flower
Hold Infinity in the palm of your hand
And Eternity in an hour
William Blake, poet, painter and print maker (1757-1827)

'It is not the critic who counts; not the man who points out how the strong man stumbles, or where the doer of deeds could have done them better. The credit belongs to the man in the arena.'
President Theodore Roosevelt, president of the United States of America (1858-1919)

'Our deepest fear is not that we are inadequate. Our deepest fear is that we are powerful beyond measure. It is our light, not our darkness that most frightens us.'
Marianne Williamson, author, spiritual teacher and lecturer (1952-)

'We make a living by what we get, but we make a life by what we give.'
Winston Churchill, statesman, and British Prime Minister (1874-1965)

'Comparison is the Thief of Joy.'
My second quotation from Theodore Roosevelt

2. I know many find it corny, and it does have an old-fashioned feel to it, especially in the last line, but a rich source of inspirational quotes is the poem 'If' by Rudyard Kipling. Lines which are particular favourites of mine include:

If you can meet with Triumph and Disaster
And treat those two impostors just the
same;

And

If you can trust yourself when all men
doubt you
But make allowance for their doubting too.

3. On the page opposite is the outline of a bookmark. Fill it with an inspirational quote that resonates with you.

4. Alternatively, make up your own inspirational saying and write that down instead.

5. Cut out the bookmark and laminate it if you want to. Having it in your book is a constant reminder of its positive message.

(38.)

LEARNING TO ADAPT

I am just back from a trip to a museum in Duxford, outside Cambridge. I had made a plan with my host to meet at the station, but waited on the wrong side of the platform, in the wrong car park, so I missed my lift. Time was ticking away, and it seemed as if I was going to be late. I was worried that I would be letting down my host. So I plucked up the courage to ask a train official who was driving out of the car park if she knew where the museum was, secretly hoping she might offer me a lift. And she did. A happy ending despite an unpredictable beginning. The experience prompted me to reflect on how much I like my travels to go according to plan.

Most of us prefer to follow a more predictable path and don't like being rattled by unforeseen events. And, unfortunately, life feels especially unpredictable at the moment. The world is going through rapid and unprecedented change. We might in the past have relied on certain pillars of stability, be they religious, political or familial. Such sources of security have gone for many people and so too has the sense of a job for life.

The problem then is how to accept unpredictability, and become more flexible, just as I was forced to today. Because the more rigid our map of the world, the more opportunities there are for that map to collide with the messiness of our reality. The reason I remained relatively calm throughout my Duxford adventure was a realisation that struck me a few years ago: life never, ever, goes exactly as planned. Best throw away that map. Or, as I read in an Instagram slogan by Rachel Wolchin: 'My entire life can be described in one sentence. It has not gone according to plan, and that's okay.'

The trick is to choose how to respond to this inevitable diversion from what we expect. One answer is to decide that actually much of life's excitement can reside in the unplanned. We are forced to be alert in order to figure out new ways forward. In the process we learn. The days when my plans are derailed are more memorable than the days when life goes on course.

A second idea is to imagine your thoughts in cartoon speech bubbles, placing in each bubble the fixed outcomes to which you were attached. So in this case, that I would be met at the station, that I would get to the conference on time. Then picture reaching out your hand, and gently popping the bubble, thereby allowing space for a new reality. You can make this even more concrete by drawing the bubble on a piece of paper.

Learning to be more adaptable in small ways has in turn helped me cope with bigger, more important unpredictable events. My life has not gone to plan. And that's okay.

Your turn to deal with moments that require adapting to unforeseen circumstances:

1. The bubble method: this is best if you don't have access to a pen or paper.

● Next time you find yourself in a situation that is not going according to plan, stop and close your eyes.

● Imagine your thoughts as a bubble. Inside that bubble, collect up all your thoughts about what was supposed to have happened.

● Then imagine reaching out your hand, and popping the bubbles that include all that is no longer going to happen. Imagine the bubbles dissolving, and all those outcomes no longer existing, dispersing and vanishing into tiny drops.

● You now have the space to adapt more calmly to the new reality that is no longer competing with your fixed assumptions about what should have happened. Say to yourself, 'Life doesn't go according to plan – and that's okay.'

2. You can do this same exercise with a pen and paper, which makes it even more concrete.

- Write inside the speech bubble above the fixed outcome to which you were attached and had to abandon, as life didn't go according to plan.

- Cut out the speech bubble.

- Scrunch it up.

- Throw it away.

(39.)

REFLECTING ON YOUR ROOTS

We are back from a perfect autumnal day of picnicking and fruit picking with friends. Collecting up the Cox's Orange Pippins reminded me of my late grandmother: one of my favourite places was her garden, where we spent many happy hours filling baskets with fruit from the assorted trees she had planted.

The experience is bittersweet. On the one hand, remembering my granny makes me feel melancholic. I miss her, yet how many people now remember her apart from me? In the greater scheme of things, we are all insignificant. Who remembers even more famous figures? Think of the celebrities who lent their names to streets around the world, such as Sir George Downing, the 17th-century diplomat and treasury secretary after whom London's Downing Street is named, or Baron Haussmann, after whom the Boulevard Haussmann in Paris is named and who carried out a huge programme of urban renewal of Paris's boulevards in the 19th century. In a hundred years or so, Donald Trump will be a similarly obscure figure from the past.

On the other hand, I do remember my grandmother. Thinking about her lends me welcome perspective on my own life. Yes, my work is important, but family members are more so. In particular, my granny was there for me when I needed support at vulnerable moments. She was the one who made me chicken soup and massaged my sore neck.

Creating a family tree is one way of reminding ourselves of the debt we owe our families. Of course, not all relations are equally influential or indeed supportive in the way my granny was, even if they do merit a place on the tree. A family tree can be as much about letting go of toxic family relationships as much as reminding ourselves of positive ones. Even when we are close to our families, those we are related to can push our painful buttons more often than anyone else. As Leo Tolstoy's character Levin says in *Anna Karenina*: 'On entering family life he saw that it was utterly different from what he had imagined. At every step he experienced what a man would experience who, after admiring the smooth, happy course of a little boat in a lake, should get himself into that little boat. He saw that it was not all sitting still, floating smoothly; that one had to think too, not for an instant to forget where one was floating; and that there was still water under one, and that one must row; and that his unaccustomed hands would be sore; and that it was only looking at it that was easy; but that doing it, though very delightful, was very difficult.' Even this awareness of the very difficulty of family life can help us be less reactive.

I am also aware of those who have challenging family backgrounds: some readers will not be in touch with their families, or not have had families at all. If this is the case, you might wish to remind yourself of good friends and kindly people in your life. You might also be inspired by the poet Mary Oliver, who writes in her poem 'Wild Geese' about the sense of belonging we can find in nature:

Whoever you are, no matter how lonely the world offers itself to your
   imagination,
calls to you like the wild geese, harsh and
   exciting –
over and over announcing your place in the family of things.

My family tree served a second purpose. It helped me understand more about myself. Much of who we are today was shaped for us, not by us. The person that you are right now, reading this, this was highly influenced by past events and experiences. We are all subject to a genetic inheritance over which we have little or no control and is of such complexity it's almost like a tornado surrounding us. Just knowing this can make us gentler and more accepting of our own nature. For example, thinking about one relation who suffered from low moods made me understand that there is probably at least a partly hereditary explanation for my depression. On a cheerier note, I now realise how my love of gardening comes from my apple-tree-growing granny, who was always bent over her spade.

Your turn to derive perspective from considering how your family has influenced you:

1. Fill in your family tree below. Use as many boxes as you need given the extended nature of many families today, and create spaces for all the different family members who have influenced you.

2. Reflect on the positive ways in which family members have influenced you and write them down in the speech bubbles below. They may not be close family, but could be distant aunts or cousins. If this is challenging, which it may be, try writing down two or three friends who have influenced you positively. You might also note down elements of nature which influence you in a positive way – perhaps the way trees give us shade and produce fruit; or the way seas and rivers give us places to swim and feel alive.

3. Reflect on those family relationships which have been less positive and see if you can let them go. You could use the breathing exercise on page 14 in the *Learning to Adapt* chapter to help you do so.

4. Below are five empty boxes. Imagine these are the main buttons your family push in you. Again, see if you can let them go.

5. Choose a few of your own characteristics, and see if you can trace them back to your own relatives. List the relative on the left, and the characteristics on the right.

Relative	Characteristic

THIRD
APPRECIATION
PAUSE

Rethinking difficult people

You are well over halfway. Well done! Now for another way of thinking, this time about challenging people.

This is about becoming less censorious of others. Many of us tend to be overly critical, because our brains evolved with a negative bias, as we established in *Feeling good enough* on page 159. In that exercise, I discussed feeling critical about ourselves. This appreciation pause is about being less critical of others. This might seem an overly narrow focus, but given how much of our wellbeing is affected by our social relations, it is an approach worth adopting before you prepare yourself for the next gear.

The problem is that when we voice our irritations about our fellow humans, we tend to feel worse. After a brief moment of self-righteous release, we increase the attention we are paying to a person's downsides. This makes it harder for us to feel connected with others. Research suggests that the more positive we are about others, the greater our satisfaction with the relationship.

Every time you find yourself moaning about somebody else, see if you can neutralise that negative thought with something to be appreciative about them instead. This is a hard challenge for most of us. Hell, as the philosopher Jean Paul Sartre said, is other people.

Next time you start sounding off about someone, stop. Instead, begin with a dose of being kind to yourself. We all have these judgmental thoughts. You might like to adopt what the psychologist Carla Croft describes as a 'knowing smile' technique. This means something like 'there I go being human again', or 'that sounds familiar, yes, I have criticised or complained about x or y person before'. It is about first acknowledging how human it is for judgmental thinking to creep in.

After that, we can make wiser choices about what to do with our castigatory thoughts. Sometimes I find it's enough to adopt Croft's knowing smile and let the complaining thought pass through as meaningless mental chatter. Or to pinpoint an aspect of the person's character to praise instead. I find I usually feel much calmer about those that irritate me after I pause to think about them in this way.

Adopt this new, less critical way of thinking before it is too late. The Duke of Wellington was asked in old age if he could have his life again, was there any way in which he could have done better? He answered: 'Yes, I should have given more praise.'

HITTING THE HIGHER NOTES

(40.)

RETHINKING MISTAKES

Recently, a friendly neighbour I have known for a while told me she had been much criticised in her annual work appraisal by a boss she feels doesn't like her. She's been miserable since. Meanwhile, I too have had what feels like a dramatic setback: arguing with a relative, which has left me gloomy. For both of us, tea and sympathy is not enough to deal with our respective senses of failure. We are now sitting at my kitchen table, making small black boxes instead.

When planes crash, recovery teams try to work out the cause from the on-board flight recorder. Doing so helps them improve safety standards for the future. In the same way, we too can imagine psychological black boxes when we metaphorically crash. After all, the Chinese word for 'crisis' is made up of the symbols for danger and opportunity. Rather than thinking in terms of negatives or positives, instead crises can give rise to opportunities. Our successes can make us clever, but our setbacks can make us wise, as my grandmother used to say (and as perhaps yours did too).

It is a big part of modern education to help children see that without mistakes there would be no learning or deepening of their relationships with each other – what psychologists call a 'growth mindset'. Less 'win or lose' and more 'win or learn'. If a fight were to happen in the playground, hopefully both parties would be asked how they had contributed and possibly what could be learned.

But then as adults we often tiptoe around, making sure bust-ups never occur. Yet rows can be like storms. They end, and sometimes in their aftermath, the air can smell sweeter than before. We can miss the richness of that experience, which yields gifts and is normal and healthy. Often we are so worried about offending others, that some of our relationships lack authenticity. There is no authentic relationship that doesn't require the word 'sorry' sometimes.

This exercise makes learning from our mistakes easier by making it a ritual, involving two people. If we discuss our reality with someone who has a different perspective, we're more likely to be able to rethink our setbacks in a more positive way.

So here I am with my neighbour, cutting out bits of paper and having fun glueing them together to make boxes. The glueing and sticking brings us together. Focusing on the craft allows us to chat in a new way: somehow our two dramas feel less frightening and more manageable as we work side by side. We both feel less alone and learn from each other. We are doing this thing together.

(I am conscious at this point that you may be reading this and thinking, 'Well, I don't have a supportive friend to do this with.' In which case, by all means do this exercise on your own. You may find having done it once gives you the courage to ask someone to do it with you next time.)

I am admiring the little boxes we have made, though they don't look much like flight recorders. In reality, the ones on planes are confusingly bright orange to aid in their recovery after accidents. Our boxes are not as indestructible and are made out of black card. But we are both doing the exercise in good faith and imagining our box is like the one used on an aeroplane.

The next step is to pop notes into our homemade boxes through the letterbox space at the top we have cut out. These notes sum up our joint thoughts, and what we have both learnt from the perspective of someone else. As this exercise is reserved for evaluating dramatic, rather than everyday failures, we needed time to chat things through. The actual writing part of the exercise was quick: both the mistake and the lesson learnt were only a few words each as the work had gone into the conversation beforehand. On one side of the paper we have written out our mistakes, while on the other we have noted briefly what we might learn from them.

My neighbour's first mistake was poor time management: she struggled with deadlines. The lesson we both decide on that is she needs to deal with her habit of procrastinating. Mine was to fail to communicate clearly with my relative. I need to be more assertive (see page 222). And so, we continued. My friend also needs to discuss her work schedule with her manager. She needs to be more open about the pressure she is feeling and reassign some of her work when she's overwhelmed.

The longer we keep going, the easier we find the process. We realise that nearly all the important scenes in our lives seemed at the time to be our lowest points. Yet so often low points are turning-points. Some universities in the US even run programs in 'Failing Well' and invite students to create CVs of their failures. I like the Black Box method as the fact that we are both popping notes into the same box and acknowledging mistakes makes the process easier still. We all make mistakes!

And on we go, until we both get tired and give each other a hug. I write out one final slip of paper in capital letters. 'You are loved for who you are, not just your achievements or for how you perform, nor are you blamed for making a mistake as we all do, all the time.' Sometimes tea and sympathy have their part to play as well as putting small bits of paper into a home-made box.

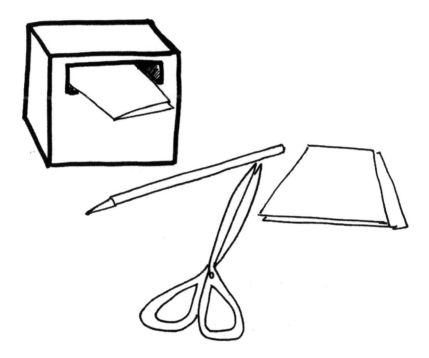

Your turn to reframe situations using a black box:

1. Ask a friend if they will do the black box exercise with you. As you will be helping each other, they don't have to be a close friend, just someone you feel comfortable with. You can also do this exercise on your own.

2. Use this template to cut out your own black box. Trace it on a piece of black card if possible. Fold it into a cube, secure with glue and cut a posting slot.

3. Now, on a small piece of paper, use three words to describe your mistake. One word to describe the setback, one word for the way it makes you feel, one word for the lesson you learnt.

4. Post your cards into the box, fold them up if necessary.

5. Throw away or recycle this box with your mistakes inside. You have dealt with them by reframing them in a positive way.

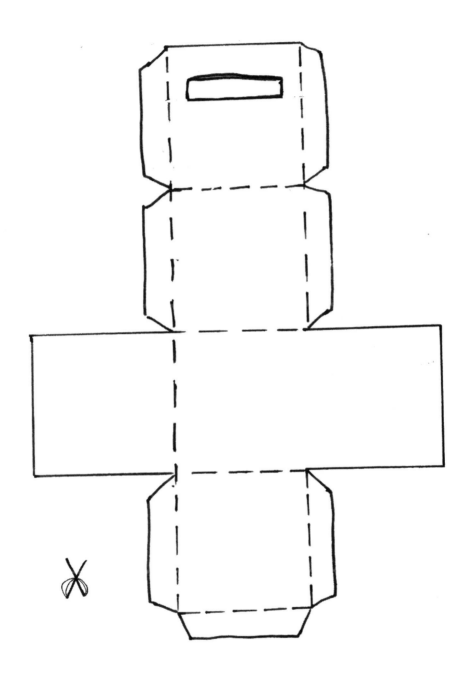

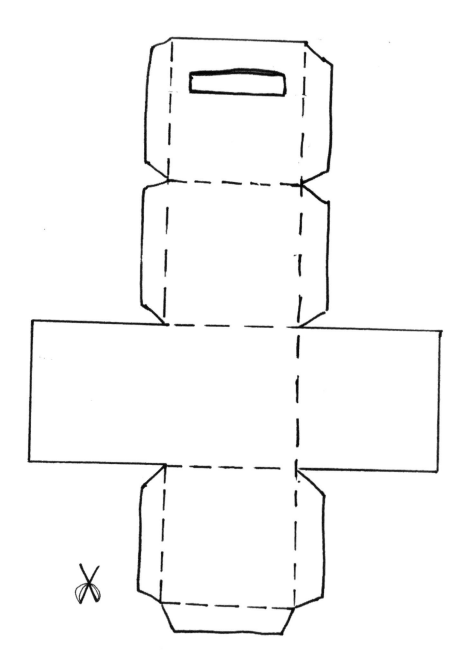

FINDING YOUR PURPOSE

Today I have discovered a new word. It's *ikigai*, an ancient Japanese expression that loosely means 'a reason for living'. I came across the term at a wellbeing workshop. A group of ten of us were chatting about how having a sense of purpose can make us feel more joy. It's not just what we do, but why we do it that makes a difference to our wellbeing: the residents of the Japanese island of Okinawa are among the world's longest-living people and say finding their *ikigai* has been one secret for their long and fulfilled lives.

Ikigai can sound like a grand thing that's impossible to achieve. I felt inadequate when I heard others in the group talk about their *ikigai*. One person talked about his life as a teacher, which sustained him even when his job was stressful: his *ikigai* was to make a difference to his students. When he started talking about his pupils, he visibly came alive.

A second man talked of his love for his family and being a dad: that was his *ikigai*. A taxi-driver said his purpose was to give his children a university education, not having gone to university himself.

Others in the room however were more like me and less sure what their *ikigai* was. A military veteran said he struggled to feel the same sense of purpose in his civilian job. This experience is common, and we are especially vulnerable to feeling a lack of purpose in retirement.

But there is no need to panic. You may have your *ikigai* without knowing it. Here's how to break down the concept into four smaller challenges:

- Do you have something you love doing? (This can include hobbies.)
- Do you think the world needs something?
- Could you be paid for anything?
- Are you good at anything?

Ideally, an *ikigai* needs all four elements to work. When we broke down the question into these four smaller parts, all of us had a few boxes ticked, which tempered our earlier sense of lacking purpose. Phew. When you complete the exercise overleaf that breaks the question down, even if you can only complete a few bits of it, you are doing well.

Your turn to use ikigai to feel fulfilled in life:

1. Close your eyes and think for a few minutes before you answer the following questions:

- What do you love? (Passion)

  ....

  ....

- What do you think the world needs right now? (Mission)

  ....

  ....

- What can you get paid for? (Profession)

  ....

  ....

- What are you good at? (Vocation)

  ....

  ....

2. Then, with the list of answers above, see if you can find anything that fits all four by using this interlocking Venn diagram. Sum up your own *ikigai* in the centre of the Venn diagram opposite.

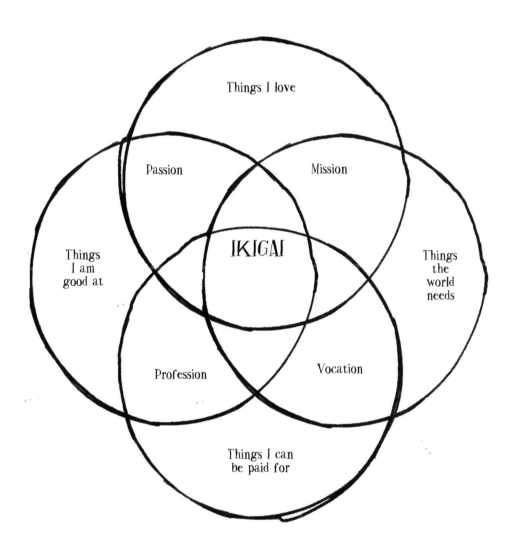

(42.)

MANAGING TIME

I have been over-trading during the last few weeks: the term comes from the world of finance and refers to a company that expands its operation too quickly, without the resources to match. I feel as if I too don't have the capabilities to meet all the fresh demands piling up at work, and at both ends of the family spectrum. I am sorting stuff for the new school term and looking after my father who has had a rotten tooth taken out. He can only eat puréed food and doesn't like the cauliflower mush I have made.

How then to find more hours in the day and become the calm and loving daughter I wish to be? I use lots of different methods. Sometimes it is best just to say no. Easier said than done for people pleasers like me. I often fall into the trap of saying yes without thinking. But it has been life-changing to say no in a kind, respectful and honest way. It can take considerable courage to do this, but the breakthrough came when I considered the other person. My father might have preferred me never to have offered to make lunch, than to do so with such ill grace.

Having some ways of saying no at the ready helps too. My favourites include:

- 'I'd love to do this but I can't take on any more at the moment.'
- 'I don't think I am the best person to help on this Dad, but can I find someone else who might help you with lunch?'
- 'I'd rather say no to meeting you for a lunch now than say sorry later when I can't deliver.'
- 'I would love to meet up but the reality is that I am over-committed for the next few weeks. Can we make a plan then?'
- And best of all, use 'don't' rather than 'can't', as in 'No thank you, I don't stay up late in the evenings' rather than 'No thank you, I can't stay late in the evenings'. 'Don't' gives us agency and power, whereas 'can't' implies that something has been imposed on you and you are not allowed to do it.

Once I feel safe with 'no', I am clearer about the meaning of yes. I use my 'yes to this, no to that' system. This has brought clarity to how much time I am devoting to something at the expense of something else. For every dilemma, I weigh up the fact that, if I agree to that, I am saying no to something else. So, if I say yes to looking after my dad, that means I am saying no to giving myself some time to recharge by walking the dog. This is sometimes known as the 'opportunity cost' of any given dilemma: by choosing one thing, we give up something else. This has allowed me to say no to unfulfilling yeses – and in turn made my diary more manageable.

Another way to get on top of my diary is to reduce the number of decisions I take each day altogether. Decisions make me anxious, as I imagine there is a perfect resolution out there. Worrying about whether I have made the right decision uses up even more precious time.

Decisions cause anxiety because we have too many of them every day. Neuroscientists call the information we hold in our working memory 'cognitive load'. Many of us are overwhelmed by the large flows of information that bombard us via email, smartphones and social media. Even small decisions can be just as mentally costly as making more important ones. Every choice we make can drain us, both physically and mentally.

As we have seen, sticking to a daily routine can help, in the same way that Steve Jobs wore a fresh black turtleneck from a pile of identical black turtlenecks every day (see *Dressing* on page 20). This saved his energy for bigger decisions. Habits like these also provide anchors of certainty, which reduce anxiety (though black turtlenecks are not for me). The same holds true for moral decisions.

Finally, the Urgent/Important grid, developed by the businessman Stephen Covey, can be helpful. Covey suggests we are more likely to be waylaid with short-term issues that feel urgent, but actually we are better off deciding whether something is important longer term. He puts relationship-building, recognising new opportunities and planning in this category. All of which depend on having time, so if you can ever delegate or use money to save time, do so. Research shows people report improved mood when they spend money on time-saving ways rather than material goods. Planning a list of things to do for the week in this grid, reproduced on the next page, can help you prioritise and make better decisions. Doing so made me realise I did have time to make some carrot purée. And my Dad liked it.

Now your turn to practise saying no:

1. Write down some of your own phrases which will make it easier
for you to say no:

… …

… …

… …

… …

… …

… …

… …

… …

… …

… …

… …

2. Fill in some examples of your own to get into the Yes/No decision-making habit to manage your time better. I have included some examples to give you an idea of how to do this.

Yes To This	No to that
If I say yes to spending hours on trawling through all my emails ...	... It means I will be saying no to reading a proper novel that might prove insightful and lift my spirits and make me rethink a few things
If I say yes to having one too many drinks ...	... It means I will be saying no to sleeping well, waking bright and early the next day, and making the most of my Saturday
If I say yes to staying late at work ...	... It means I will be saying no to finding the time to watch a movie and to relax and unwind

3. Write a list of things to do for the coming week:

… …

… …

… …

… …

… …

… …

… …

… …

… …

… …

… …

… …

… …

… …

4. Try and place each item on your to-do list in one of the
four quadrants.

Urgent and important:	Important but not urgent:
Urgent but not important:	**Not urgent and not important:**

(43.)

CONSIDERING WHAT YOU WANT

A warning! This exercise is about writing your own obituary. Of all the exercises it is among the most Marmite-like: the one which has provoked strong responses, both negative and positive. Some older people who've tried this exercise said looking back in this way provokes regret, and they found it uncomfortable, scary even. Meanwhile, some younger people said it was challenging to write about their life when it had only recently begun. They preferred the exercises in the book that look forward rather than look back.

But others said this exercise was helpful. It can clarify the kind of people we want to be in the years that remain to us, and emphasise that we are the writers of our own narratives. As always, the rule is see if the idea appeals to you and ditch it if it doesn't.

I was inspired to do this exercise myself after I went to a memorial service. After the eulogy, I sat quietly in a wooden pew on a small red cushion at the back of the church. I imagined what I would like to hear said about me when I died. What sort of person did I want to be remembered as? I was not preoccupied with things I might or might not have achieved, which is what obituaries normally focus on, but rather on the values by which I do or don't live and by what I've done or haven't done for others.

My thoughts tumbled out. I decided the thing I was most proud of was my match-making prowess: I had introduced my sister and my sister-in-law to their respective husbands. I decided to order my thoughts by writing my own obituary, adapting the regular structure that such notices follow.

An obituary is usually about 800 words. The first third or so is devoted to why the person was deserving of notice. The second two-thirds is a trot through the person's life, including when and where they were born and educated, and highlights of their career, up to their death. The last couple of paragraphs summarise their contribution to the world, and focus on their achievements and successes. I decided to mimic this structure, except instead of listing worldly achievements, my own obituary would focus less on ambition and more on my connections with others.

Contemplating our death can help us focus on what matters in life. There are only two days in our lifetime that are shorter than twenty-four hours – the first and the last. While we celebrate our birthday, thinking about the day we die can also be worthy of celebration if it makes us see life as precious and short.

The exercise seemed timely as life seems to have sped up. As Shakespeare said, 'I wasted time, and now doth time waste me'. What values do I want to live by in the years that remain? If death seems a long way off, imagine you have three months to live, to galvanise your thoughts on what matters to you. Or borrow the Bhutanese habit and think about your death five times a day: the surest path to happiness, they believe, and an intriguing correction to the Western culture of imagining we will all live forever.

When I got home, I wrote out my own possible obituary. The exercise was tough: it gave me a jolt to think I didn't have all the time in the world to become the calmer, kinder person I want to be, assuming that I am lucky enough to live for another 20 years or so. My strongest observation was how the days have rushed past and are now gone. That was my life. My fear was less of the death we all face, but of not truly noticing the days I am living now.

So, writing your own obituary can yield two results. First, it shows you a snapshot of your life to date. Second, reflecting on your past in this way is a powerful spur to action and a jolt into a life which more closely reflects the person you want to be. What is not written is as important as what is. Frightening or inspiring? You decide.

Your turn to write an inspiring obituary:

Use the prompts to help you along:

FIRST THREE PARAGRAPHS

.... was best known for their qualities of ....
....
And made a difference to
....
....

NEXT EIGHT PARAGRAPHS – SCENE-SETTING

She/he was born in ....
....
And grew up in
....
....
(Your name)'s family included ....
....
....
....
....

(Your name) was a loving mother/father/sister/brother/cousin/
friend/partner to

....

....

....

....

Those who knew (your name) acknowledged these qualities about
her/him ....

....

(Your name) lived a life exemplifying these values ....

....

(Your name) will be remembered for making a difference to

....

....

(Your name) was proud of these moments in her/his life ....

....

FINAL TWO PARAGRAPHS

(Your name)'s life was about

....

....

....

....

PS. And if you enjoyed this exercise, you might consider doing the
same exercise, but this time write about someone else. Don't save
your kind words for someone's eulogy after their death, but express
what someone has meant to you in their lifetime.

MAKING A CASE CONSTRUCTIVELY

Arguments are generally horrid, but those at work are especially hard as there is less of the extra slack usually given to us by our friends or family. Take a recent exchange I had with a colleague. We disagreed on what to include in a presentation on nutrition. Both of us wanted the final say on the choice of slides. Should they include pictures of vibrant fruit and vegetables? Or scientific studies? I was for deep purple plums and emerald green broccoli, she not. Neither of us would back down. My old reactive brain got the better of my steadier cognitive new brain and I was angry, sad and fearful all at once. Whisper it, but I even shouted.

Given that peaceful relationships make me happier than practically anything else, it clearly pays to avoid such rows. After this altercation, I chatted through what had happened with a psychotherapist. She shared the following SUPA method of having more productive conversations when tempers are fraught and rows are in the offing. This is slightly different to having an assertive conversation (see *Having assertive conversations* on page 22)

as it assumes conflict is likely from the start. The example here shows how I might have handled my dispute at work. But the formula could equally apply to a row with a friend or relation.

All the steps are about trying to reach a satisfactory outcome for you both. So before you even begin, consider what you hope will happen. Then set the tone in as conciliatory and positive a way as possible. Be careful with your opening remarks. Start with: 'I might be wrong about the choice of slides, but...' or, 'You might be right, but...' This acknowledges how your colleague feels. Usually sentences beginning with 'I' are better and less accusatory than those beginning with 'You'. This is also a good moment to gently mention feeling hurt or that you see things differently. Or that your effort towards a project has gone unacknowledged.

Use specific examples. This will help to identify exactly what the issues are. Avoid generalisations and use specifics. For example, 'I think it would help participants in this case if we included some slides about the power of omega 3s, the healthy fats. These slides would, I feel, be particularly good', rather than 'The presentation would be better if I chose the slides'.

Be Positive. Stress what you like about someone's work or ideas, not what you dislike. Find points of agreement. This is especially important when tempers are fraying. Focusing on common ground makes disagreeing about other things easier. Rather than saying, 'I don't like it when you want to run presentations entirely your way,' I could say, 'I appreciate all the work you have put in, and I like some of your slide choices.' Try and keep things impersonal. It's about the work, not the person: one is changeable, the other less so.

Throughout the discussion, ask questions instead of making assumptions. You might want to repeat back what the other person has said, and then add, 'It seems like you are feeling x or y. Is that right?' Always give the other person the opportunity to correct your assessment. It's noteworthy what kind of assumptions we make when we feel threatened – not least that the other person will see things as we do. Our minds make leaps that have little to do with the reality of the situation. Honour the fact that the other person is being true to their self.

All of which would have helped us have a more constructive chat about our slides. Super, if I say so myself.

Your turn to make a case constructively

1. Before you begin – what outcome do you want from your chat? Is it important for you to have a row?

2. Then follow the SUPA method:

How could you... set the tone?

....

....

....

....

....

....

How could you... use specific examples?

....

....

....

....

....

....

How could you... be more positive?

....

....

....

....

....

Could you ask...?

....

....

....

....

....

ESCAPING YOUR COMFORT ZONE

A coldish evening and I am back from a class on how to give a presentation, cradling a mug of celebratory hot chocolate. Even the thought of the lesson had given me the heebie-jeebies. I had fretted that I would make a fool of myself by freezing and forgetting my words. Humiliation is one of the most powerful emotions, and humiliating moments are often those we find hardest to forget. I did not want to be embarrassed. But I went because avoiding what I am frightened of usually only makes it worse. The best way to overcome my fears is to find the courage to face them, hard as that can be. As Eleanor Roosevelt supposedly said, do one thing every day that scares you.

So that's why I found myself in a group of ten students and longing to be back home, cuddling Sammy in front of the telly. But my mood began to change thanks to a sympathetic tutor dressed in an inviting apricot kaftan. She told us how we would overcome our fears and move out of our comfort zones by practising in baby steps. We would adopt the Pre, During, and After method – or the PDA approach (no, not as in a Public Display of Affection!). First, the Pre. This meant we would prepare for the presentation. We would remind ourselves of our purpose in being at the workshop, and how we would talk to a friend who was feeling nervous. We would practise in front of a mirror and in pairs. We were advised to use some relaxing standing exercises to steady ourselves. (See *Sitting and standing* on page 43).

Then the During stage, when we would present to all the strangers in the class. During these first two stages, we were supposed to stick with any anxious feelings, accepting the discomfort until it gradually dissipated and using breathing exercises if need be. The more we did this, she said, the more we would build up what psychologists call our 'distress tolerance' – our ability to withstand negative emotions or distressing states. We could even reframe anxious feelings as energising and arousing instead.

Then, in the After stage, we would discuss how we felt our about presentations and any other techniques we might include to improve them.

Her method worked. I was able to face

the group without a pounding heart when I did my own presentation, and learnt much in the chat afterwards. Going forward, our coach suggested that we could continue our journey out of our comfort zones by listing those situations that fill us with fear, or those we avoid. So in my case, that might be giving a presentation to 20 people rather than the ten I had faced that night. We should list these scenarios from least scary to most frightening. Then we should build our confidence by tackling the easier ones first. If you begin with something too challenging, you might just give up all together. In addition, in the absence of a coach like her, was there anyone else who could support us as we embraced new challenges?

Understanding why we prefer to stay in our comfort zone can also, counter-intuitively, make us more adventurous. We humans are loss averse. We dislike loss far more than we like an equivalent gain. Such a cognitive bias probably kept us safe amid the dangers of the African savannah, where the downsides of taking risks were as big as the lions on the prowl. But there are dangers in not being a risk-taker: our ancestors also benefited from variety, whether of habitats, food or mating partners (though this is not an excuse for infidelity!)

In fact, the American educational psychologist, Carol Dweck, argues that we need to adopt a 'growth' rather than a 'fixed' mind-set: if something is hard, then that's a good sign as it shows our brains are growing and adjusting. We need to question our self-imposed limits on what we can achieve and expand our horizons. We imagine that when we are thrown out of our usual comfort zone, all is lost. But it is only then that what is new and good often begins. And that includes a mug of hot chocolate afterwards.

Your turn to face your fears and challenge yourself when you would rather watch telly or talk to your pet:

1. Write on the dartboard the activities you will try that are out of your comfort zone. The more frightening the situation you face, the more points you receive. Think of it like a dartboard, only this time you aren't aiming for the bull's eye. You may find it daunting to think of as many as three different challenging situations, so just start with a 10-point activity if that feels more comfortable and perhaps come back to this exercise in a few weeks' time.

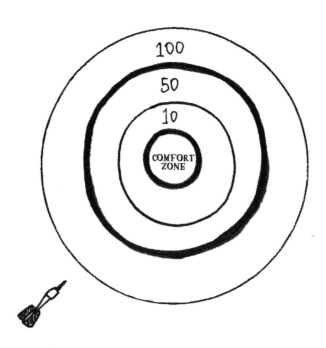

2. Now choose a 10-point activity from your dartboard opposite to ease yourself into this process. Here is a reminder of the PDA method. Have a think about the questions below and then plot your own PDA on the steps in the image on the next page.

The Pre stage – How you will prepare before the activity

- Why are you doing this?
- Is there a way of practising ahead?
- How would you reassure a nervous friend who was contemplating something outside their comfort zone?

The During stage – How you will prepare for doing the actual activity

- Using breathing to stay steady (see *Belly breathing* on page 19).
- Accepting difficult feelings and letting them dissipate

The After stage – How will you make the most of having found your courage?

- What you have learnt
- What you might do differently next time
- Adopting a growth mind-set going forward

On the steps below you can plot your own PDA (explained on previous page). In each step, list the strategies you will use to manage the fear of moving out of your comfort zone.

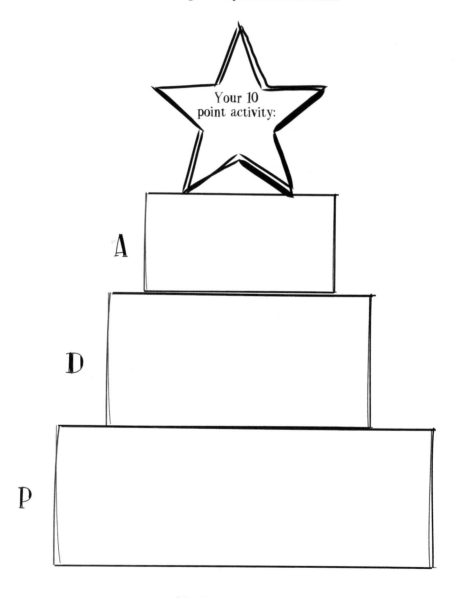

Your 10 point activity:

A

D

P

3. Is there a friend who could support you through this challenge and help you face your fears? Use the table below to name the person who could help you, the activity they can help you with, and how they are going to do so.

NAME ....

ACTIVITY THEY WILL HELP ME WITH

....

....

....

....

HOW THEY WILL DO SO

....

....

....

....

(46.)

CHALLENGING MIND-WRITING

Yesterday, I was driving slowly around a carpark looking for a space. As I circled, I noticed a young woman in a dark navy Mini waving at me. Why was this woman trying to bother me? Was she trying to nab the space ahead of me which had just come free? I felt angry. The woman must be hostile. I needed to respond to some kind of threat. I grabbed my handbag that bit closer to me. Then she wound her car window down and told me my lights weren't working. I almost crashed with relief.

Once safely parked, I realised I had in fact fallen into several heffalump thinking traps. In both cases, my old instinctive brain had taken over and I had been hijacked by strong emotions. The first trap is when we succumb to 'over-alert' thinking. This is when we are over-sensitive and quick to imagine others are hostile. Veterans often struggle with this, as they find themselves hyper-vigilant, with an overdeveloped fight-or-flight response.

Linked to over-alert thinking is the second trap of imagining that we can read the minds of others. In fact, usually we have no idea what others are thinking. Our 'mind-reading' is actually more like 'mind-writing'. We write a narrative in our heads of what we assume the other person is going through. The control-freak boss may be anxious about losing their job; the demanding relation may be feeling powerless and taking it out on you; the person who doesn't answer your text may have just found out their daughter is unwell, as happened to me last week. The speeding car beeping its horn may be a desperate man driving his pregnant wife to hospital.

In addition, we also write a story about our own reactions. My typical kind of mind writing is that I have done something wrong and someone doesn't like me. This often happens when someone doesn't reply to a text or email and I imagine I have offended him or her in some way. But sometimes, and less often, the process can work in reverse. I assume someone will be nice and they are the opposite.

How then not to fall into these kinds of thinking traps? One approach is to remember there's always a space between what you assume, and how you respond. The problem is it's often a tiny space, and we can let our assumption fill it. To hollow out that space and give you more room to reduce over-alert thinking and mind-writing, acknowledge your instinctive brain at work. Then question its assumptions.

The second stage is to become more aware of how inaccurate we often are about the story we then tell ourselves. The best way to do this is to start keeping a record of when we have run away with a bit of over-alert thinking or mind-writing in the past and not got it right.

Yesterday's carpark exchange would be an example, although in this case I quickly realised my mistake, as the woman corrected my assumptions within seconds of me making them. On other occasions, I can mind-write for weeks before I realise the error of this thinking style. Keeping a historic record has shown me how often I am inaccurate, and what a high emotional toll this can exact.

Your turn to think freely instead of creating assumptions:

Use this table to examine three examples of times when you have jumped to conclusions and fallen into the mind-writing trap in the past. The exercise is about recalling those times when you were not accurate about other people, and how much making assumptions cost you emotionally.

Who did you make wrong assumptions about?			
What did you tell yourself that person was thinking?			

Did you suffer in some way because of the narrative you created?			
What turned out to be a more accurate portrayal of the facts?			

FINDING YOUR TEAM

One thing I missed when I first got back to work after having my children was being part of a team. Initially, I only felt up to writing on my own, and it can be lonely scribbling away. I was used to the camaraderie of a newspaper office. Over time, I have been able to enjoy the pleasures of teamwork thanks to collaborations with companies and charities, teamwork that I had to seek out actively given the isolation of a writing life.

How does teamwork make us happy? Well, it can give us purpose. (See *Ikigai* on page 189). Whether you are one of three or 30, every team member is a cog in a machine that can't function without them. Teamwork is about dividing up roles, meaning the sum is greater than the parts. It gives us a lovely sense of resolve when a group comes together in order to achieve a shared goal.

Teamwork also makes us feel needed. In the famous theory of a hierarchy of needs developed by the psychologist Abraham Maslow, he said that we have a need to feel loved and to belong, as well as other more basic needs such as those for food or shelter. When other people think you matter, this helps you believe you matter too. And you do matter! You really do, as others can't work without you.

Thirdly, working alongside others liberates us. We can forget about ourselves when we shift our focus outwards, embracing the people around us with humility. What a relief.

All well and true. But it takes skill to be a good team member and to care more about the team winning than about scoring a goal yourself. I have become a better team player by becoming aware of the characteristics of bad ones. A colleague described the two toxic 'Cs' to watch out for if you wish to be a team player: criticising and complaining. If you find people avoid partnering with you, or you are not included in team plans, keep a note of how often you criticise, especially behind someone's back. Spend less time complaining about someone to someone else, and more time talking to them yourself.

Secondly, note how often you control others. You may think you know best, but you will never know what others may be capable of if you don't allow them creative freedom. This is just as true at home when it comes to letting others take charge in the kitchen, for example. I have struggled with teamwork when it comes to how I want the house to be run. As has my husband when it comes to how I load the dishwasher.

Another way of becoming more of a team player is to ... join a team! You become a team player by literally becoming a team player. Put yourself with others who partake in a shared goal. This is exemplified by how the charity, The Felix Project ,works, an initiative that collects nutritious food that cannot be sold. Some volunteers need friendly smiles to persuade shops to donate food just past its sell-by date. Other volunteers need to be good drivers to deliver the food to the right charities. Others need to be efficient organisers. It really is a case of teamwork makes dream work, as different people with different skills play their parts.

Finally, you might like to find an image that sums up teamwork for you. I like the picture conjured up by this old Hasidic tale. In one room is a large round table, in the middle of which sits a big pot of stew. Yet the people sitting around the table look famished. Each person has a spoon with a long handle. Although the long spoons just reach the pot, their handles are longer than the would-be diners' arms. Unable to bring food to his or her lips, no one can eat. This room is Hell. In a second room, the scene is repeated. This time the people sitting around the table are plump and happy. In this room, the people have learned to feed each other with the long spoons. This room is Heaven. Or, as the tale doesn't say, a place where teamwork is in action.

Your turn to find your team to help prove you matter too:

1. Divide up this circle into a pie chart. Estimate how much of your time you spend criticising, controlling, giving creative space to others or praising them.

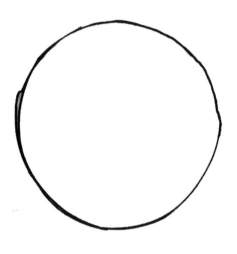

2. Divide up the pie chart again, thinking about how you can be more of a team player.

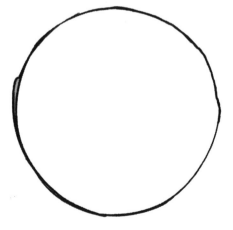

2. Are there any teams you might join?

- Sports teams?
- Charitable teams?
- Teams at work?
- Family teams?

3. Is there an image which sums up being part of a team for you? Draw it below.

(48.)

FLEXIBLE THINKING

In the past, there was something of a stigma in writing about mental health. But times have changed, and I have been writing about being anxious for a while now. I feel relaxed about doing so. But there's another taboo subject that is only now being talked about: our hormones. Whatever age, at some point hormonal changes will affect us. Such moments often coincide with anxiety. We see this in adolescents, in post-natal women and in menopausal women and andropausal men, all of whom are vulnerable to mood swings.

My own menopausal hormones are not proving helpful at the moment. My mood swings have exacerbated my tendency to think in an extreme and absolutist way, also known as black-and-white thinking or sometimes as dichotomous thinking. This is when we perceive things, and people, as either wildly positive or deeply negative. One second we feel elated, the next despairing; one moment we want to work all night, the next to watch telly forever. People are fabulous, darling, or simply awful. There's nothing in-between these extremes, no nuance or shade of grade.

Actually, I can't just blame my stage in life. I've always had something of a tendency to this kind of absolutist thinking, and plenty of others think in this extreme way, whether they have learnt that behaviour or they were born that way.

In the past, this tendency to oversimplify and see others as either bad or good may have helped our ancestors judge who would help them in emergencies. But if we take this way of thinking to an extreme, evidence suggests it may play a causal role in depression. We feel dismayed as we have imposed our own inflexible demands on the world and the people in it. Both fail to meet our expectations, whether positive or negative. One study analysed language used in various online anxiety and depression forums and found a higher concentration of absolutist words like 'everything', 'constantly', 'completely' and 'nothing', which are characteristic of black-and-white thinking.

GPs and health professionals recommend we use some of the ideas of cognitive behavioural therapy (CBT) to overcome dichotomous thinking. The first step is to become more aware of your own cognitive style and if you are slipping into this type of either/or thinking with never a shade of grey. Watch out if you find yourself either being mad keen on something, or simply hating it, be it a colleague in the office or a work project. Beware of comments like 'I just can't stand x or y.' Equally, notice if you start to become opinionated, and unable to acknowledge different viewpoints. Finally, keep an eye on moments when you find yourself checking out altogether.

If this feels challenging, one of the best ways of modifying faulty thinking is to keep a thought log, which is rather like the worry log earlier in the book (see *Managing worry* on page 65). I have given an example overleaf whereby you examine your extreme thought, how you might challenge it, and what a more moderate thought might look like. It's an approach that anyone can use to question their thoughts, whatever the challenge they are tackling, and whether their hormones are playing up or not.

Your turn to question your black-and-white thinking:

Below is a table to examine how you can moderate your thoughts. I have filled in the first three entries to give you an idea of how you might do this. Add in some of your own black-and-white thoughts on the page opposite, and then consider how you might imagine a more balanced and subtle way of thinking.

Thought	Challenge	Moderation
I might as well quit my job.	Who is suggesting I leave my job? Are there aspects of my job I am good at? Have others acknowledged things I do well at work?	I can cope with staying at work, even if I sometimes feel uncomfortable and as if I am no good.
I am no good at writing articles.	Am I the best judge of my own work? Do I often find myself being critical of my work? In the past, have my judgments been correct or faulty?	I have just written some lousy sentences, but I have also written some good ones, and I need to keep writing and practising to improve.
I think I was rude to my partner.	Did anyone say that? No one is perfect.	I do sometimes say intemperate things but I also make a point of doing kindly actions.

Thought	Challenge	Moderation

(49.)

HAVING ASSERTIVE CONVERSATIONS

I am in the garden deadheading the remaining cerise geranium flowers and snapping the tops of the faded creamy white roses, rehearsing a chat I have been avoiding. I hate endings, but I need to move on from a working relationship which no longer feels right. Like many who can be anxious, and who aim to please, I can find talking in a straightforward and assertive way hard. I am fearful I might come across badly. But if I fail to be truthful and direct about how I feel, I risk being stuck in an unfulfilling partnership. On a trickier note, I also need to sort out our financial relationship to the satisfaction of both of us. My ideal is to balance valuing the outcome (ending the relationship and coming to a financial settlement) and valuing the relationship (I would like to stay on good terms). If I value the outcome too highly, I risk losing the relationship. But value the relationship too highly and I risk not getting what I want.

For me assertive conversations are less about avoiding rows, though of course

there is an element of this (see my chapter on *Making a case constructively* on page 200). Instead, they are more about communicating straightforwardly about things that matter to me and where there should be no need to come to blows. Through trial and error, and with a particular debt to a barrister friend of mine, the psychologist Ashley Conway, and the work of Marshall Rosenberg's theory of Nonviolent Communication, I now have a format that helps me handle these exchanges.

My first point is that it is best to meet face to face. Emails and texts are for less significant exchanges. Having said that, an email or text may be an important first step to say you are planning to have an important conversation. All too often, unassertive people plan to have an important chat and then back down the moment they arrive. If the 'we need to talk' text is already out there, it cannot be taken back.

Face the person you are talking to, standing with confidence and an open posture. (See *Sitting and standing* page 43). Then speak a bit more slowly than you usually would. When we are feeling out of control, our voice tends to jump in volume and pitch. Such a voice suggests anxiety rather than assurance. In contrast, a steady (pause) deliberate (pause) voice (pause) conveys confidence in conversation. In addition, speak softly. The 13th-century Persian poet, Rumi, wrote: 'Raise your words, not your voice. It is rain that grows flowers, not thunder.'

Then, having a structure to the conversation helps you stay on track, makes you less likely to get emotional or forget important points, and more likely to express yourself strongly and clearly. Just as I advised in my earlier chapter on *Making a case constructively*, you should use the first person, 'I', and then say what you are feeling. Part of the point of the chat is to be truthful about your emotions rather than to repress them.

So, in my conversation about my work relationship, I might say I feel I have changed, the relationship has run its course and I need to move on. Opening up and sharing your feelings in this way can stop you from sounding too aggressive or overly confident. But it is best not to dwell on your feelings, as this can make you look overly vulnerable. Balance wins the day. In advocacy, there's also a theory that you shouldn't stress your point too much. If you do, the effect may be to put off the judge, because it seems to them like you are trying to force the point across, and they react against that, like twin poles of a magnet.

Always say what you would like the other person to do in a calm way. So: please can we formally end our contract, as from today, in a written email. In addition, can we find a way to end our financial relationship too that is fair to both of us.

At this point, the conversation shifts from being about what you feel and want, to what the other person feels. This is the key pivot. It's important for them to feel you are also listening to them, otherwise you will simply be aggressive rather than assertive and risk losing the relationship altogether. Start to use thoughtful, gentle questions, along the lines of, 'Is this acceptable to you?' What you require may, or may not, be acceptable to the other person. You might use the word 'willing', as in 'are you willing to accept this financial settlement?' As part of a research project. Elizabeth Stokoe, professor of social interaction at Loughborough University, analysed thousands of hours of recorded calls from customer services to mediation hotlines and police emergency calls. And found that the word 'willing' seems to have a magical effect on people.

If it's not something they are willing to do, then it's time to pause while you work out the next steps and what will be acceptable to you both. Spaces in conversation always help to make the other person feel respected. If, for example, the other person is upset by what you have said, you might say at this point something like, 'This isn't the conversation I meant to have,' or, 'I wasn't expecting you to say that. Instead of giving you an immediate response, can I have a minute to think?'

Once you have adjusted your offer, or they have adjusted theirs, which of course may take some time, the final question is, 'Do I have your agreement?'

Conducting an assertive conversation is not easy, which is why I have a format and I rehearse it beforehand. If you fail to prepare, then you should prepare to fail. In my case, my preparations led to a happy outcome, and the added bonus of a tidier garden.

Your turn to practise having an assertive conversation:

1. I feel that ....

....

....

Say more about what exact emotions you are feeling

....

....

2. I would like you to ....

....

....

....

3. Is my request acceptable to you? Are you willing to do so?

4. Take a pause if need be to re-think your request.
- Formulate a request you are both happy with
- Ask if you have their agreement

(50.)

ALIGNING VALUES AND GOALS

In the past, I have spent little time thinking about the topic of values. Instead, I have concentrated on getting through each day in one piece. But recently, my health has improved, and my age has advanced, to the point where a little deeper reflection is in order. One thing I have started doing is to list the values that matter to me. I then ask myself whether I feel my goals at home and work, and the hobbies I pursue, tally with the values I actually believe in.

So here I am, chewing on a blue biro as I get my thoughts in order. Not as easy as it sounds, listing values. I try hard to think about what I feel is important and what I care about, as opposed to values I have absorbed and which have been passed on to me by others, especially by my family. Sometimes our values are so ingrained it is hard to identify where they came from in the first place.

Two ways of thinking have helped me clarify my values. First that values tend to be long term and can underpin a lifetime's endeavours. Second, there is nothing life and death moments to remind you what really matters: imagine you only had one day left to live. What would you do? Spend it with your family? Then family values are important to you. Complete that novel? Then creativity and hard work are values that matter to you. Help a child from a disadvantaged background? Then caring for others matters to you.

You might wish to jot down values that matter to you in different spheres of your life – namely your values at work, at home and in your community, as well as in your leisure time. On my list, my values at work included trying to help others; at home, they included trying to be a good daughter and mum; under community they included trying to be polite and cheerful. Note the trying.

Having established my ideal values, I then made a note of how I actually spend most of my waking hours: what current goals do I pursue? And what hobbies do I engage in during my leisure time? Goals can be targets we want to achieve, so a goal is to be promoted or hired on that project, or to buy that car, for example. They can be short term, but they can also be longer term – a goal to help disadvantaged children, for example, could be one you maintain for your entire life.

Armed with my two lists, the next step was to see the extent to which I was staying true to my values in how I was actually spending my time. We tend to be most content when our goals and hobbies stay true to, and align with, our values. This kind of dovetailing can lead to a richer life too. In my case, I am lucky in that my work of writing about mental health is rewarding as it fits well with my values of trying to help others. I need to make some adjustments in my home life, however. Thinking about goals and values has made me realise that I need to spend a bit more time with my children if I wish to live a life true to my value of being a good mum.

You can apply the same principle of aligning values and goals when it comes to your hobbies, which may be easier to adjust than changing job. For example, if one of your values is to look after yourself physically, set yourself the goal of joining an exercise class or playing football. In my case, I would rather walk our dog Sammy. Enough of goals and values, time for a trip to the park.

Your turn to live out your values through your goals :

1. On the left side of the table, list the values that matter to you. Ask yourself what would you do if you had one day left on earth? What matters to you most? You could list your values:

At work
At home
In your community
In your leisure time

2. On the right-hand side of the table, list your goals and hobbies. Again, you could list your goals:

At work
At home
In your community
In your leisure time

3. See to what extent your lists match up by drawing lines between them. This is a good way of seeing whether your goals and hobbies agree with your values. If they don't, over time think about tweaking them so that they dovetail more fully.

VALUES	GOALS and HOBBIES

(51.)

AFFIRMING YOURSELF

Creating affirmations provides some of the same mood-boosting benefits as turning to inspirational quotes, but there's a difference between the two. Affirmations are designed to be just about you, whereas an inspirational quote expresses a generalised wisdom or a received truth. It is the difference between saying 'I am patient' and 'Patience is a virtue.'

It follows that there's a creative element to making up your own affirmations. You are not borrowing someone else's words, but actively thinking up your own bespoke sayings, according to what you need to plant in your subconscious. There's strength to be found in creating your own narrative in this way.

I use several kinds of affirmations. The first type are the phrases I turn to when I feel I have messed up. Perhaps my inner critic is busy, and I need to hear the voice of my inner friend instead. (See *Feeling good enough* on page 159). I use verbs such as learning, growing and practising in order to attach a gentle, kindly tone to whatever value or quality I aspire to. So a typical phrase might be, 'I am always growing as a person even if I am some-

times less kind than I would like' or, 'I am practising saying no even if I don't always manage to do so and sometimes let people down.'

A second type of affirmation would include phrases for those days when all we can do to find peace is to tell ourselves it is okay not to be at peace. So 'It is okay to be sad,' or 'It is okay to feel rattled that my mum is unwell.'

My third category of sayings affirms my ability to look after myself as best I can. These ones often begin: 'I give myself permission to...' I then add a verb like 'look after', or 'care', and end with a nurturing activity. So one such affirmation might read: 'I give myself permission to care for myself by taking a nap.' I use these when I need to take a break, and they could be anything from watching a box set to going to bed early. Of all the affirmations I use, 'I give myself permission' is the one I use most.

For all types of affirmation, I make them positive and realistic, using the present tense, and then practise saying them out loud. I found this hard at first, and was even more self-conscious when I said my affirmations out loud in front of a mirror. But research has shown that those who repeated a set of four compassionate phrases while looking at themselves in the mirror produced the highest levels of positive emotions and lower levels of self-criticism compared with those who didn't. Speaking aloud in this way focuses my attention and reconnects me with my own voice: most of us only use our voices to communicate with others, not ourselves. By practising ahead, the affirmations will be lodged in your head when you need them in a hurry and every time you pass a mirror you can repeat them (assuming no one else is watching!).

While reading your affirmations, notice your tone. You may find it moves from sounding weak and frightened to stronger and more composed. You might also try this exercise sitting cross-legged on the floor, a pose that evokes childhood and thus readiness to learn. Sitting down also signals to your body that you are not preparing to run, so your body relaxes and you enter a more receptive state.

It is interesting to notice which ones you find hard to say. In this way, affirmations may provide useful information about areas you need to work on for your own psychological growth. And I give myself permission to do so.

Your turn to give your self-compassion a boost with affirmations:

1. For your first type of affirmation to silence your inner critic, good verbs to use include: learning, practising, growing, developing. If you can, and it is challenging for many, write down some affirmations of this sort below.

E.g. 'I am practising being more patient, even if I don't always succeed'

....

....

....

2. For your second type of affirmation, for when it is hard to find anything to feel settled or calm about, start your sentence with the phrase: 'It is okay to feel not at peace about...' Write down some affirmations of this type below:

....

....

....

3. For your third type of affirmation, which is about developing a kindly voice to yourself, begin with phrases like, 'I give myself permission to...' or, 'I will allow myself to...' Choose from phrases that express self-compassion, such as:

- Look after myself
- Take care of myself
- Nurture myself
- Love myself

Write down some of these affirmations in the space below:

....

....

....

- When you have written out your affirmations, say them out loud, or to a mirror. Spend a moment looking at your reflection. Notice how it feels if you bring a gentle smile or friendly expression to your face. As you say your affirmation, direct feelings of care and warmth to your reflection.

- Write out all the affirmations on separate slips of paper, put them in a jar, and pull one out each day. Try and live that day according to the affirmation you have chosen.

(52.)

QUIT COMPARING

As the saying nearly goes, comparisons have always been odious, but never more so than in the age of social media. Navigating the digital world is so challenging that this is the very last exercise of the book! It can seem as if other people's successes are constantly thrust upon us in a stream of photos, videos and messages. We are all complicit in the great digital game of curating perfection. I know I try and show myself in a good light on my own Facebook account and Twitter and Instagram feeds.

Yet when we compare ourselves with others, we often fail to remember that they too are signalling perfection. We believe that they lead shiny, glossy lives, which makes us feel inadequate ourselves. Social media acts as a giant incubator for insecurity and self-doubt, as we are constantly exposed to the sight of other people seemingly having a good time. As Chekhov's Ivan Ivanovich says: 'We see those who go to the market to buy food, who eat in the daytime and sleep at night, who prattle away, merry... But we neither hear nor see those who suffer, and the terrible things in life are played

out behind the scenes.'

Unsurprisingly, such negative feelings aren't good for us. Resenting what others have makes us unhappy both over the long term and in the moment.

How then can we stop ourselves feeling inadequate? Social media, or those we follow, can't make us feel anything. We decide how we interact and how we feel about those on social media, just as we do in real life. If we imagine we are forced to feel a certain way by our interaction, then we give away all agency in how we respond. (See also *Taking back control* on page 155). We can make choices about that response. And those responses are changeable.

I can feel both negative and positive when I interact with social media, depending on the day. In general, I feel best when I remember that I am looking at the way someone wants to portray themselves. I am sure like all of us they too have rows and tricky dynamics. Who doesn't?

A second helpful attitude I find is to remember we are all equal. We are all subject to the same levellers, be they poor health, suffering or, ultimately, death. All of us humans happen to be sharing this planet at this exact moment in history and are in this together. That's why the second exercise is for you to fill in your own social profile, as well as someone you admire.

A final step is to use social media with considerable care, taking time to deflate its impact by being deliberate about the company we keep online. Be wary of randomly looking at those for whom you feel a corrosive envy. Instead, proactively seek out genuine stars who can become role models in a rather lovely, old-fashioned way.

For example, you might choose to look at Michele Obama's profile on Facebook in which she describes herself as 'Girl from the South Side, and former First Lady, wife, mother, dog-lover. Always hugger-in-chief'. Of course, being a dog-lover, she's my kind of person. Her own inspiration is her husband Barack Obama, who in turn sums up his philosophy by saying on his website: 'You have the talent and the power to improve the lives of your fellow human beings.' I feel my better self when I read that.

Engaging with someone whose goals and mind you admire, rather than how someone looks, can make you more likely to achieve those same goals. Concentrate on someone's inner attractiveness rather than their appearance. The company of those you admire will leave you feeling galvanised and energised to follow their example. Psychologists describe looking up to others in this way as 'emulative envy', which is a good thing.

It's even better to spend time face to face with those we admire, though I don't think the Obamas have plans to meet me any time soon. But if I can, I seek out my role models, going to hear them speak if they are well known.

Not all my pin-ups are famous: one is my mother, another the peer-support worker at a local charity. In general, my heroes tend to have some of the qualities I lack at times but wish to practise more regularly. They are calm, they listen, they let others speak, and they are trying to make a difference to others. One day, I want to be more like them. There is always more to learn...

Your turn to see others with more admiration and less jealousy on social media:

Decide below on someone who is a role model for you and fill in some details about their life that inspire you, as well as a photo or drawing of them if that's easy.

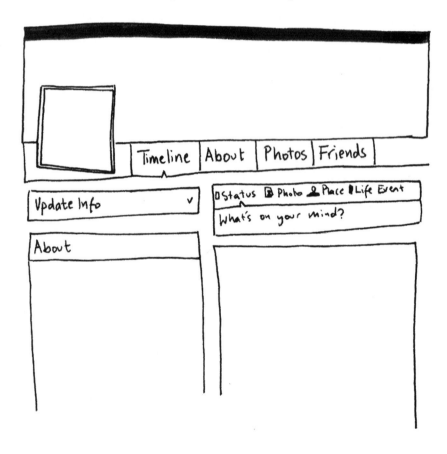

Then do the same for yourself, rewarding aspects of your life that you are proud of. Also annotate your image with your situation when the photograph was taken. Was all as perfect as it seems? The likelihood is that the problems and insecurities of others are also hidden behind a pretty picture.

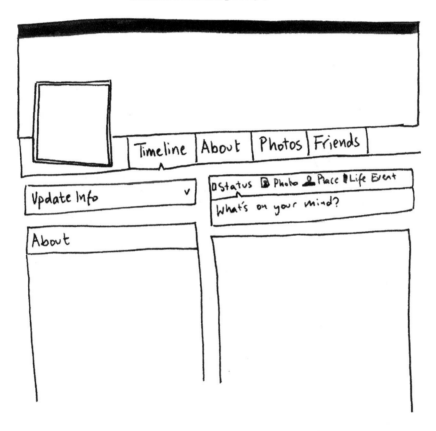

Next time you encounter someone you feel jealous of, write down two challenges they have faced to remind yourself of our common humanity. You may find that when you next see this person, you pick up on these positive characteristics more than you used to.

Remembering everyday moments

Phew! Congratulations. You have finished. My invitation is now for you to wind down by once again thinking of anything you appreciate, starting with yourself. You might find this phrase useful: 'I extend a hand of kindness to myself...' which in turn helps me realise how lucky I am and how much I appreciate many other things in my life. Being kind to ourselves sets us up for appreciative feelings.

In my case, feeling self-compassionate allows me to appreciate our 14-year-old son doing the washing up without being asked; my husband for nipping to the shop first thing one morning so we had enough milk for breakfast; the clematis coming into flower near our front door; the good sleep I had last night; the colleague who stayed late one night to finish a project we were working on. There is no moment too small to appreciate. While you appreciate yourself and then other things, take a few breaths as you do so. Well done. And thanks for keeping me company.

THE BACK OF THE BOOK:
CONNECT

You have come to the end of the book and I hope you are not feeling too exhausted by the sheer number of my suggestions. I hope that even just one or two activities speak to you, and that you can incorporate them into your daily life and sometimes sing in the rain. I have shared all things that hold me up in the year and help me through as a package. Taken on their own, some of the ideas may sound small, but put together in a toolbox they have empowered me to take charge and to feel calmer and more peaceful. They are all fragments, but together I hope they make a kind of whole.

At this stage, you might like to think about the three practices that most resonated with you, and that will be ready and waiting at the top of your toolkit, to be plucked out as need be. Perhaps there are some ideas you want to try again, and explore a bit more? Or three activities you might want to recommend to someone else? To solidify everything you have read and tried out in *Singing in the Rain*, you might remind yourself of the goal setting on page 226 and commitment cards on page 94.

Finally, I hope the book will be a source of help and inspiration going forward. Looking at the illustration opposite, place any left hand finger on the left circle and any right hand finger on the right circle. This will complete the circuit. Feel the energy flow through you like electricity, up your left arm and down your right arm. Imagine you are radiating warmth just as a light bulb does when its circuit is complete. Focus on anything in the book that has made sense to you. Give yourself a moment to run through the ideas and activities you might try and practise regularly, and write them below. Return to this page when you need reassurance that you are the one with the power in your life.

I will try these activities:

1.

2.

3.

4.

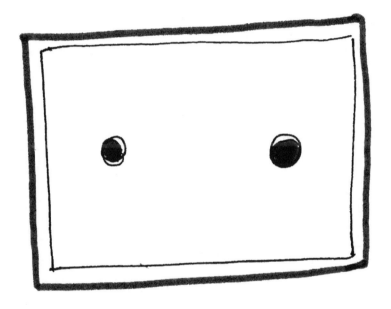

Thank you!

Author Biography

Rachel Kelly is a former *Times* journalist, writer and mental health campaigner. She is an ambassador for SANE, Rethink Mental Illness and The Counselling Foundation. She lives in London with her husband and children.

Other books

Black Rainbow: How Words Healed Me – My Journey through Depression
Published by Yellow Kite Books (2014)

Walking On Sunshine: 52 Small Steps to Happiness
With illustrations by Jonathan Pugh.
Published by Short Books (2015)

The Happy Kitchen: Good Mood Food
Published by Short Books (2017)

This book was born of the interaction with readers and those I have met online, as well as through my workshops and talks. My thanks to you all! I would love to hear your ideas for feeling peaceful, calm and happy, so many of which have helped me already. Please connect and share any thoughts with me via:

Email: rachel@rachel-kelly.net
Twitter: @RachelKellyNet
Instagram: @rachelfkelly
Facebook: @rachelkellynet / Rachel Kelly – Writer, Public Speaker, Media Commentator
Website: www.rachel-kelly.net*
*where you will find more Singing in the Rain resources: some poems, stuff about how our brains work, as well as the studies and books that helped me to write this workbook.

Acknowledgements

I am grateful to all who have lent me their time, expertise and support during the writing of this book. Special thanks go to the fantastic Short Books team of Aurea Carpenter, Catherine Gibbs, Helena Sutcliffe, Evie Dunne and Rebecca Nicolson, and it has been a pleasure to collaborate with the brilliant cartoonist Jonathan Pugh. I would also like to thank my friends and colleagues Oliver Chittenden, Carla Croft, Miranda Devas, Eliza Hoyer-Millar, Sallyann Kreizer, Dr James Le Fanu, Elena Langtry, Neill Lunnon, Dr Greg Lydall, Dr Paquita Marrin, Constance Marquis, Tara Maxwell, David Montgomery, Liam O'Brien, Serena Oppenheim, Professor Carmine Pariante, Judith Perring, Alexander Reviakin, Susanna Scouller, Andy Walton, and Mark Williamson. I am also hugely grateful to those who got in touch via my mailing list and those who have come to my workshops. Thank you to all those from mental health charities who provided valuable feedback, in particular Nia Charpentier at Rethink Mental Illness, Anna A from Depression Alliance, Jonathan Robinson and Antalia Terblanche at SANE and Kinga Kwiecinska at the charity SMART. Finally, most of all my gratitude goes to my family who put up with my singing in the rain, badly.

CENTERING YOURSELF	BELLY BREATHING	RISING EARLY	DRESSING	SMILING AND LAUGHING
VISUALISING	MOVING	EATING FOR CALM AND FOCUS	SITTING AND STANDING	RELAXING PHYSICALLY
ENJOYING SIMPLE PLEASURES	PLAYING LIKE A CHILD	CHANTING, GARGLING AND HUMMING	MANAGING WORRY	BEING KIND TO OTHERS
FINDING PERSPECTIVE	COLOURING	BEING HAPPY NOT PERFECT	SOCIALISING AND FRIENDSHIPS	EMBEDDING NEW HABITS
WRITING A LETTER	LISTENING TO MUSIC	TRAVELLING TO A JOYFUL PLACE	CREATING SPACE FOR NEGATIVE FEELINGS	FINDING THE POSITIVES
CELEBRATING	TAKING A PAUSE	BALANCING ROLES	SEEING AFRESH	TREE CLIMBING

SKETCHING NATURE	FINDING FLOW	BEING A FRIEND	WRITING POETRY
TAKING BACK CONTROL	FEELING GOOD ENOUGH	DISCOVERING INSPIRATION	LEARNING TO ADAPT
REFLECTING ON YOUR ROOTS	RETHINKING MISTAKES	FINDING YOUR PURPOSE	MANAGING TIME
CONSIDERING WHAT YOU WANT	MAKING A CASE CONSTRUCTIVELY	ESCAPING YOUR COMFORT ZONE	CHALLENGING MIND-WRITING
FINDING YOUR TEAM	FLEXIBLE THINKING	HAVING ASSERTIVE CONVERSATIONS	
ALIGNING VALUES AND GOALS	AFFIRMING YOURSLEF	QUIT COMPAIRING	

Use the symbols below to record which practical steps resonate with you – or don't – as you progress through the book.

Works for me ✔

Recommend to a friend ♡

Not for me ✗

Unsure, maybe try again ?

If you are experiencing a mental health problem of any kind, you can contact the charity SANE. Their helpline called SANEline (0300 304 7000) is open 4.30 p.m.-10.30 p.m. daily.
For more information, visit SANE's website: www.sane.org.uk

BLANK PAGES

Please use these pages for notes, doodles, or completing some of the activities within this book. Enjoy!

BLANK PAGES
249

BLANK PAGES
251